flavours of **Morocco**

flavours of **Morocco**

delicious recipes from North Africa

Ghillie Başan

photography by Peter Cassidy

RYLAND
PETERS
& SMALL

LONDON NEW YORK

Dedication

For my mother, with all my love.

First published in the United Kingdom in 2008

This edition published in 2011
by Ryland Peters & Small
20–21 Jockey's Fields
London WC1R 4BW
www.rylandpeters.com

10 9 8 7 6 5 4 3 2

ISBN: 978 1 84975 086 8

A catalogue record for this book
is available from the British Library.

Printed and bound in China.

For digital editions visit
rylandpeters.com/apps.php

Design, art direction and prop styling
  Steve Painter
Senior Commissioning Editor Julia Charles
Production Paul Harding, Toby Marshall
Art Director Leslie Harrington
Publishing Director Alison Starling

Food Stylist Ross Dobson
Indexer Hilary Bird

Notes

• All spoon measurements are level, unless
otherwise stated.

• Eggs are medium unless otherwise specified.
Uncooked or partially cooked eggs should not
be served to the very old, frail, young children,
pregnant women or those with compromised
immune systems.

• Ovens should be preheated to the specified
temperature. Recipes in this book were tested
using a regular oven. If using a fan-assisted
oven, follow the manufacturer's instructions for
adjusting temperatures.

• To sterilize bottles and jars, wash well in
soapy water, rinse throughly, then boil in plenty
of water for 10 minutes. They should be filled
as soon as they are dry, and still hot. (If the
preserve is cold, let the bottle or jar cool before
filling.) For more information on preserving and
food safety, go to: http://hgic.clemson.edu/food.htm

contents

the flavours of Morocco

Colourful, decorative, sensual and scented – a feast for the senses. The food of Morocco reflects a fascinating mix of the cultures that have left their mark on the region: the indigenous Berbers with their traditions of tagine cooking and couscous; the nomadic Bedouins from the desert who brought dates, milk and grains; the Moors expelled from Spain who relied heavily on olives and olive oil and brought with them the Andalusian flavours of paprika and herbs; the Sephardic Jews with their preserving techniques employing salt; the Arabs who introduced the sophisticated cuisine from the Middle East along with Islamic culinary restrictions; the slaves from central Africa with their tribal secrets; the Ottoman influence of kebabs and pastry making; and the finesse of the French.

Moroccan cooking is regarded as the most exquisite and refined of the Maghreb – the North African region comprising Morocco, Tunisia and Algeria. Known as 'the land where the sun sets', the Maghreb provides a stunning geographical and culinary door to the rest of Africa, as well as a lively mix of the European and Middle Eastern influences that have shaped its culinary history. From the impressive mountain ranges and the majestic cities of ancient dynasties to the southern deserts with their date-palm

oases and the extensive coastlines fringed with sun-drenched beaches, Morocco is a land where the medieval and the modern are atmospherically intertwined. This is true of the culinary culture too – medieval recipes with modern twists – a unique blend of the sensual and the exotic.

The kingdom of Morocco is rich in produce with fertile coastal plains and lush valleys fed by the streams that flow from the melting snows of the Atlas Mountains. With a climate and topography similar to California, it is blessed with resplendent harvests of olives, figs, oranges, lemons, melons, aubergines, peppers, tomatoes, courgettes, pulses, grains and wheat, as well as good grazing for sheep and goats. When the Arabs first invaded the region they described it as 'paradise' as their eyes swept over the productive landscape of extensive orchards, vineyards and fields of grain. The Romans before them had been driven by a similar sight as they conquered the agriculturally savvy Carthaginians and developed the wheat production and the fruit and olive cultivation in the land they named Mauretania.

The Arab invasion, which came in waves between the seventh and fourteenth centuries, brought about the biggest changes to the Moroccan culture. Not only did they influence the culinary culture with eastern spices, such as cumin, ginger, cinnamon and saffron, from their far-reaching trade routes in the Indian Ocean, as well as the notion of sweet and sour with the fruit-inspired dishes of ancient Persia and the sophisticated cuisine of Baghdad, which was the medieval capital of the Islamic Empire, but they also converted the population to Islam and the Arabic language. With the adoption of this new faith came the culinary restrictions associated with the slaughtering and preparation of meat, as well as special foods and dishes required for the various religious festivals, such as Ramadan, the holy month of fasting, and Aid el Kebir, the celebration of the near-sacrifice of Ismail (Isaac in the Bible).

The French, who colonized North Africa at the end of the nineteenth and the beginning of the twentieth centuries, also had a lasting influence on the culinary culture. Nicknamed the *pieds-noirs*, 'black-feet', by the Arabs, who coined the expression from the sight of the highly polished boots of the soldiers, the French brought soups and sophisticated fish dishes, café culture, wine-making, and their own language to the region. Along with the French immigrants who spread themselves all over North Africa, there also came a wave of Italians to Tunisia and Spaniards to the northern part of Morocco.

Many of the French immigrants settled in the new, sparkling white city, Casablanca, with its wide avenues and busy markets and remained there immersed in an Arab culture, but leading a very

French way of life, until the 1960s when Morocco gained independence and they were forced to leave. Culturally, they joined ranks with the Sephardim, descendants of the Jews who had been expelled from Spain and Portugal at the end of the fifteenth century, who had settled mainly in Fes, Marrakesh and Essaouira on the coast. As a result, the *pied-noir* cooking created its own identity, combining French roots with Jewish dietary laws, and all the dishes were given French names, most of which survive today. After the 1960s many of the *pieds-noirs* resettled in similar climes along the Mediterranean coast taking with them the very thing that identified them with Morocco – their unique cuisine.

Each region and city has its own culinary influences: in Tangier and Tetouan, they are Andalusian, Mediterranean and Ottoman; in Marrakesh and Safi, they are African and Berber; and in Fes, there is a strong mix of Arab, Andalusian and Berber. Both Marrakesh and Fes have established Jewish quarters, known as the Mellah, meaning 'salt' due to their highly regarded preserving techniques, without which the Moroccans would not have their ubiquitous preserved lemons. From a culinary perspective, Fes is regarded as the jewel in the crown. Often elaborate in style, Fassi food combines the subtle secrets of the imperial kitchens with all the cultural influences that have come and gone in the city. One of the Fassi specialities is the pigeon pie, *b'stilla*, which is reputed to be the best in Morocco – feather-light, crispy, aromatic and sweet. The cinnamon-coloured city of Marrakesh is the door to the desert and the gateway to Berber and African culinary traditions with the lively Place Djemma el Fna at its heart. Here, where gold and African slaves were once traded, the snake charmers, costumed watersellers, and story-tellers work their trade in a cloud of smoke emanating from the stoves furiously grilling kebabs and *kefta*. Not so long ago you could exchange a camel for a brace of slaves in this square, now you can tuck into a paper cone containing freshly roasted chickpeas, sprinkled with cumin and salt, and observe the theatre for next to nothing.

The labyrinthine souks of Fes and Marrakesh are the best in Morocco. With stalls and baskets full of culinary inspiration – a kaleidoscope of multicoloured spices, saffron fronds, dried fruits and nuts, preserved lemons and bitter oranges, bunches of large leafy herbs, and olives of every description – there is much to whet the appetite and caress the palette. In Fes, the most medieval city in the Arab world, there is also much to fascinate – the sheeps' heads with milky eyes, calves hooves with mud still clinging to them, runny-looking pink hearts, chunks of camel meat ready to be chopped, pasty-looking tripe draped over tables, buckets of snails and live pigeons awaiting their fate.

Food and family are the heartbeat of Moroccan culture. Much of the day-to-day life is centred around food, with visits to the markets, tea in the cafés, street snacks and religious festivals. To sample the best of Moroccan cuisine, it is essential to be invited into a home where the women of the household have lovingly prepared a myriad of tantalizing dishes. Eating on the cheap in Morocco will enable you to sample couscous, spicy tagines, savoury pastries, kebabs and *kefta*, but you will only skim the surface of the complexity and depth of flavours of the richly authentic dishes prepared in the homes. As the recipes are handed down from generation to generation, with very little recorded on paper, no two dishes will ever be the same – it all depends on the eye and the mood of the cook.

Most Moroccan meals begin with a selection of little dishes – *kemia*, *mezze* or *mukabalatt* – the name seems to vary according to the language and cultural influence. Some *kemia* dishes are simply *amuse-gueule* (palate ticklers), such as small bowls of dried broad beans, tiny slices of spicy merguez sausage, pickled vegetables, roasted pistachios and watermelon seeds, and plump olives marinated in herbs and spices; others are more complex involving cooked vegetables in salads, savoury preserves, stuffed pastries, soused sardines and mini meat balls. To follow might be a syrupy, buttery tagine served with bread, or a hearty bowl of soup. Grilled or roasted meat may be served next, followed by a mound of couscous. Fresh fruit usually completes the meal or, on occasion, a dessert, but most sweet dishes are served as offerings of hospitality, or they are reserved for celebratory occasions. Once everything has been cleared away, glasses of steaming mint tea will be served to aid the digestion while you reflect over the lengthy and wondrous meal and commit it to memory as one of life's unforgettable experiences.

aged butter
smen

Definitely an acquired taste, this fairly pungent butter is often flavoured with herbs and spices and is left to mature in earthenware pots for months, sometimes years! It is a traditional speciality of the Berbers who enjoy it smeared on bread, or used as the primary cooking fat to enhance the flavour of couscous and some tagines. It is difficult to recreate the exact taste of *smen*, but a practical recipe used in modern households gives the dish a distinct flavour, or you can substitute it with *ghee* (clarified butter), which is readily available in Asian stores.

500 g unsalted butter, at room temperature
150 ml water
1 tablespoon sea salt
1 tablespoon dried oregano

Soften the butter in a bowl. Boil the water in a saucepan with the salt and oregano to reduce it a little, then strain it directly onto the butter. Stir the butter with a wooden spoon to make sure it is well blended, then let cool.

Knead the butter with your hands to bind it, squeezing out any excess water. Drain well and spoon the butter into a hot, sterilized jar. Seal the jar and store it in a cool, dry place for at least 6 weeks.

preserved lemons
l'hamd markad

Added to so many dishes as a refreshing, tangy ingredient or garnish, preserved lemons are essential to the cooking of tagines. Of course, you can buy jars of ready-preserved lemons in Middle Eastern and African stores, as well as some supermarkets and specialist shops, but it is worth making your own. Be as liberal as you like, tossing them in salads and scattering them over your favourite tagines.

10 organic, unwaxed lemons, preferably the small, thin-skinned Meyer variety
10 tablespoons sea salt
freshly squeezed juice of 3–4 lemons

Makes 1 large jar

Wash and dry the lemons and slice the ends off each one. Stand each lemon on one end and make two vertical cuts three-quarters of the way through them, as if cutting them into quarters but keeping the base intact. Stuff 1 tablespoon salt into each lemon and pack them into a large sterilized jar. Seal the jar and store the lemons in a cool place for 3–4 days to soften the skins.

Press the lemons down into the jar, so they are even more tightly packed. Pour the lemon juice over the salted lemons, until they are completely covered. Seal the jar again and store it in a cool place for at least 1 month. Rinse the salt off the preserved lemons before using.

North African dried chilli sauce
harissa

This fiery paste is popular throughout North Africa. It can be served as a condiment, or as a dip for warm crusty bread, and it can be stirred into tagines and couscous to impart its distinctive chilli taste. This recipe is for the basic paste, to which other ingredients such as fennel seeds, fresh coriander and mint can be added. Jars of ready-prepared harissa are available in African and Middle Eastern stores, as well as some supermarkets and delicatessens.

8 dried red chillies (Horn or New Mexico), deseeded
2–3 garlic cloves, finely chopped
½ teaspoon sea salt
1 teaspoon ground cumin
1 teaspoon ground coriander
4 tablespoons olive oil

Makes roughly 4 tablespoons (a little goes a long way)

Put the chillies in a bowl and pour over enough warm water to cover them. Leave them to soak for 1 hour. Drain and squeeze out any excess water. Using a mortar and pestle, pound them to a paste with the garlic and salt (or whizz them in an electric mixer). Beat in the cumin and coriander and bind with the olive oil.

Store the harissa paste in a sealed jar in the refrigerator with a thin layer of olive oil poured on top. It will keep well for about 1 month.

kemia and salads

This classic spicy aubergine and tomato salad, which can be written as *zahlouk* or *zaalouk*, is delicious served on its own with chunks of bread, or as part of a *kemia* spread. It can be made with olive oil or argan oil, which is pressed from the nut inside the fruit of the argan tree indigenous to the Souss region of Morocco.

spicy aubergine and tomato salad
zaalouk

2 large aubergines

4 large tomatoes, skinned and chopped to a pulp

100 ml olive or argan oil

2–3 garlic cloves, crushed

1 teaspoon Harissa (see page 11)

a small bunch of fresh flat leaf parsley, finely chopped

a small bunch of fresh coriander, finely chopped

freshly squeezed juice of 1 lemon

sea salt and freshly ground black pepper

1 teaspoon cumin seeds, roasted and ground

bread, to serve

Serves 4

Preheat the oven to 200°C (400°F) Gas 6. Put the aubergines on a baking tray and bake them in the oven for about 30 minutes, until soft when you press them with a finger. Put the tomatoes in an ovenproof dish, pour over half the olive oil, and pop them in the preheated oven with the aubergines. Remove the aubergines and tomatoes from the oven and leave until cool enough to handle. Using a sharp knife, cut the aubergines in half, scoop out the warm flesh and chop it to a pulp. Skin the tomatoes, cut them in half to scoop out the seeds and chop the flesh to a pulp.

Heat the rest of the oil in a heavy-based pan, add the garlic and fry until it begins to colour, stirring constantly. Add the tomatoes and harissa and cook over a medium heat for 5–8 minutes, until thick and pulpy. Add the aubergines, parsley and coriander. Stir in the lemon juice and season with salt and pepper. Tip into a serving bowl and serve warm or at room temperature with a dusting of roasted cumin and chunks of bread.

sweet tomato purée with cinnamon and sesame seeds
matisha mhassela

This lovely, sweet tomato purée is delicious served as part of a *kemia* spread, but it is also a good accompaniment for fish and grilled meat dishes. The purée varies from cook to cook as some like to simmer the tomatoes for over an hour to obtain a jam-like, sticky consistency. Topped with crunchy, toasted sesame seeds, it is best served at room temperature with bread to dip into it.

6–8 large ripe tomatoes
2–3 tablespoons olive oil
2 tablespoons runny honey
1 teaspoon ground cinnamon
1 teaspoon ground ginger
sea salt and freshly ground black pepper
1 tablespoon sesame seeds, toasted
bread, to serve

Serves 4

Preheat the oven to 200ºC (400ºF) Gas 6. Put the tomatoes in an ovenproof dish, pour in the olive oil and bake them in the preheated oven for 15–20 minutes. Remove them from the oven and leave until cool enough to handle. Skin the tomatoes, cut them into quarters, remove the seeds and dice the flesh.

Put the diced tomatoes in a heavy-based pan with 1 tablespoon of the roasting oil. Stir in the honey, cinnamon and ginger and cook very gently, stirring frequently, for about 20 minutes, until the mixture is thick. Season with salt and pepper and tip the mixture into a serving bowl. Leave it to cool, sprinkle the sesame seeds over the top and serve at room temperature with bread for dipping.

garlicky broad bean dip
bissara

This traditional garlicky dish is popular as a dip throughout Morocco. It can also be presented as a soup, thinned with stock and served hot. Sprinkled with paprika, dried thyme or the Middle Eastern and North African spice *zahtar*, this is a delicious starter when served with Moroccan bread.

350 g dried broad beans, soaked in cold water overnight
4 garlic cloves
2 teaspoons cumin seeds
4–5 tablespoons olive oil
sea salt
a pinch of paprika, dried thyme or zahtar
bread, to serve

Serves 4–6

Drain the beans, remove the wrinkly skins and pop them into a large saucepan with the garlic and cumin seeds. Add just enough water to cover and bring to the boil for 5 minutes. Reduce the heat, cover the pan and simmer gently for about 1 hour, until the beans are tender.

While still warm, pound or whizz the beans with the olive oil to form a smooth dip. Season to taste with salt and serve warm or at room temperature, sprinkled with paprika, thyme or zahtar.

carrot and cumin salad with orange flower water
slada jazar

This is a delightful, refreshing salad that appears in many guises throughout Morocco. Whether the carrots are steamed, roasted or raw, it is always a welcome sight at the beginning of a meal, arousing the taste buds with a sweet song of tangy flavours, floral notes and a hint of cinnamon.

450 g carrots, peeled and grated
freshly squeezed juice of 1 lemon
freshly squeezed juice of 1 orange
2 tablespoons orange flower water
2 teaspoons sugar
½ teaspoon ground cumin
1 teaspoon ground cinnamon
sea salt and freshly ground black pepper

Serves 3–4

Put the grated carrots in a bowl. Pour in the lemon and orange juices and the orange flower water. Add the sugar and cumin and season with salt and pepper. Stir to combine. Cover the bowl and chill in the refrigerator for at least half an hour before serving.

Toss the salad and tip it onto a plate in a dome. Sprinkle the cinnamon over the top and serve chilled or at room temperature.

orange and radish salad with green olives
meslalla

Oranges are one of the most popular fruits in Moroccan cooking. They are used in refreshing savoury salads, tucked into tagines and served as a sweet salad with orange flower water. As a starter, sliced oranges are often combined with black or green olives and a touch of cumin, chilli or paprika in a salad commonly known as *meslalla* as well as by its literal name, *slada bortakal bil zaytoun*. This recipe is for a lovely Marrakchi variation on the ever popular theme.

3 sweet oranges, peeled with all the pith removed
12 red radishes, trimmed and thinly sliced or shredded using a mandolin
2 tablespoons green olives, stoned and sliced
2 tablespoons olive oil
freshly squeezed juice of 1 lemon
1 tablespoon orange flower water
2 teaspoons sugar
sea salt and freshly ground black pepper
a few fresh mint leaves, finely shredded, to serve

Serves 4

Cut the oranges into segments on a plate so that you catch the juice. Remove the pith and seeds and cut each segment in half. Pop them in a bowl and pour over the juice.

Add the radishes and olives and pour in the olive oil, lemon juice and orange flower water. Add the sugar and season with salt and pepper. Toss the salad lightly, cover and chill in the refrigerator for about 30 minutes.

Toss the salad again before serving and sprinkle with the shredded mint. Serve the salad slightly chilled or at room temperature.

preserved lemon and tomato salad
with capers
salade marocaine

5–6 large tomatoes, skinned, deseeded and cut into thick strips

1 red onion, cut in half lengthways, then in half crossways, and sliced with the grain

rind of 1 preserved lemon, cut into thin strips (see page 11)

2–3 tablespoons olive oil

freshly squeezed juice of ½ lemon

1–2 tablespoons capers, rinsed and drained

a small bunch each of fresh flat leaf parsley, coriander and mint leaves, finely chopped

1 teaspoon paprika

sea salt and freshly ground black pepper

Serves 4–6

There are a variety of tomato based salads that come under the banner *salade marocaine*, especially in the tourist areas. This particular recipe is a great favourite on the *pied-noir* table. Tart, fruity, crunchy and refreshing, it appears in various versions throughout Morocco.

Put the tomatoes, onions and preserved lemon in a bowl. Add the olive oil and lemon juice and toss well. Season with salt and pepper and set aside until ready to serve.

Just before serving, toss in the capers and herbs and scatter the paprika over the top.

roasted peppers with goats' cheese, onion and parsley
slada felfla wa jban

This dish can be prepared with colourful capsicum peppers, or the long, slim, red Mediterranean peppers (*ramiro*). The sweet and succulent roasted flesh of the peppers is combined with the slightly salty cheese, a crunch of sharp onion and the tangy citrus burst of preserved lemon. It is delicious served as a starter or as an accompaniment to grilled meats.

Preheat the oven to 180°C (350°F) Gas 4. Put the peppers in a baking dish, pour over the oil and pop them in the oven for about 30 minutes, until the flesh is soft and the skin wrinkly and slightly buckled. Remove from the oven and leave until cool enough to handle. Remove the stalks and peel off the skins. Cut each pepper into quarters lengthways and remove the seeds. Put the peppers on a serving dish.

Crumble the goats' cheese over the peppers. Mix the chopped onion with the parsley and scatter the mixture over the peppers. Drizzle the roasting oil over the top and sprinkle with the preserved lemon. Serve while the peppers are still warm or at room temperature.

3 fleshy, red, orange or yellow peppers, or combine all 3 colours

2–3 tablespoons argan or olive oil

200 g crumbly goats' cheese or feta

1 red onion, finely chopped

a small bunch of fresh flat leaf parsley, finely chopped

rind of 1 preserved lemon, finely chopped or shredded

Serves 4

mini fish *kefta* with saffron and coriander
kefta bil hout

One of the joys of the street food in the coastal towns, such as Essaouira, is the aroma of grilled or fried fish cooking with spices and coriander as the fish *kefta* or brochettes are prepared for passers-by. Mini fish *kefta* are often served as a starter accompanied by a salad, a dip and a bowl of olives.

450 g white fish fillets, such as sea bass or haddock, skinned and flaked

1–2 teaspoons Harissa (see page 11)

rind of ½ preserved lemon, finely chopped (see page 11)

a small bunch of fresh coriander, chopped

a pinch of saffron fronds, soaked in 1 teaspoon water to draw out the colour

2 teaspoons runny honey

1 egg

2 slices Moroccan or rustic bread, with crusts removed and bread ground into crumbs

2 tablespoons plain flour

sunflower oil, for frying

sea salt and freshly ground black pepper

1 lemon, cut into wedges, to serve

Serves 4

Put the fish in a bowl and add the harissa, preserved lemon, coriander, saffron and honey. Beat in the egg, season with salt and pepper, and add enough bread crumbs to bind the mixture. Knead the mixture with your hand and take small apricot-sized lumps into your palms to mould them into small balls. Roll the balls lightly in the flour.

Heat the oil in a heavy-based pan and fry the balls in batches for 3–4 minutes, until golden brown all over. Drain them on kitchen paper and serve hot with wedges of lemon to squeeze over them.

the olive and the argan

Without a doubt, Moroccans are the unsung olive kings of the globe. We hear about the olives of France, Italy and Greece, but when it comes to the fruit of the olive tree there are few who can beat the Moroccans for quantity, quality and diversity. Spilling out of giant plastic tubs or heaped in mounds, gleaming olives of every hue are evident at every market, around every street corner and in every home. Olives for nibbling, olives for cooking, olives for marinating; olives to be tucked into tagines, tossed into salads and baked in bread; olives to be pressed for oil or bound in preserves – the list is endless.

Of all the old market cities in Morocco, Marrakesh is the unbeatable champion of olive sellers. If you give the insistent cobra charmers of Djemma el Fna square a wide berth and move swiftly through the henna painters and the makeshift stalls of shrivelled lizards and dried chameleons, you will enter the souk and its maze of olive stalls. In amongst the jars of pickles and sheaths of mint, you will find yourself in olive heaven as you are faced with skinny, cracked green ones; plump violet ones flavoured with garlic and turmeric; crinkled black ones cured in salt; fiery yellow ones spiked with coriander, cumin and chilli; and brown, purple, orange and pink ones, as well as various shades in between. Every village has its own special combination of flavourings, each city has its own particular variety of olive, and the olive sellers all personalize their olives with their secret marinades.

With good arid soil in the coastal areas and up the slopes of the mountain ranges of the Rif and Atlas, much of the Moroccan countryside is ideal for olive growing. However, in spite of the industrious planting of olive trees carried out by the Romans – all the way from the Mediterranean coast in the north to the edge of the Sahara in the south – Moroccans grow fewer trees than their neighbours, the Tunisians, and plans for future planting of olive groves seem thin on the ground as villagers rely on the ancient, trusty trees to produce a good harvest of eating olives every year.

From mid-September to October, the green olives are picked and some are cracked and soaked in salted water, others are pitted and stuffed with almonds and pimento. The violet and beige coloured olives, which are picked in November, are often slashed with a sharp knife and soaked in brine, and the black olives remain on the trees until late November and December. As these black olives have ripened enough to be cured without having to slit the skin, they are generally rolled in salt and stored in wicker baskets which are weighted down with a heavy stone to force the fruit to weep and the salt to penetrate and crinkle the skin. The olives are left for several months then they are rinsed and laid out to dry on rooftops and terraces before being stored in oil, or tossed in a piquant marinade.

Morocco has been known to export 60,000 tons of olives in a good year and it supplies Spain and France with the bulk of their own exports. When it comes to the oil though, they are poor exporters even though the home-pressed oil is rich in colour and flavour and is delightfully fruity. This is largely due to the archaic harvesting and pressing techniques of rural Morocco where donkeys or camels still power the grinding stones, as well as the fact that there is no quality control, resulting in varied and interesting batches, but a precarious level of unpredictability. Another factor in the oil production is the reality facing rural life in many developing countries where few young people remain in the villages, preferring to migrate to the cities for work, leaving the old folk and scattered tribes to carry out the harvesting and pressing. This of course renders the local oil particularly precious and prices are rising accordingly. Although it still remains the preferred oil for couscous, many people are opting for the cheaper seed oils and for the unique argan oil from the south of the country.

Little known outside Morocco, the argan tree is thorny, gnarled and stout as it survives in dry, poor soil. A popular feature of travelling in the southwest region of Morocco is the remarkable sight of goats climbing in the argan trees and clambering along the branches to reach the fruit. There is no need to harvest the fruit, which resemble large, green olives, as the goats eat the fleshy exterior and then excrete the nut which is collected by the herders, or village women, to be pressed for oil. This process is laborious as each nut has to be cracked open to extract the kernels which are roasted before being ground to extract the oil. Argan oil, which is dark in colour with a reddish tinge and nutty flavour, is used for general cooking in the southwest region, but in the rest of Morocco it is largely sold for its medicinal and cosmetic properties. In Marrakesh, for example, olive oil is sold for cooking and argan oil is sold to soften the skin, smooth wrinkles and soothe sunburn. With increased research into its benefits, argan oil may play a key role in Morocco's culinary future. Currently, it is produced on a small scale by the regional village women who use it as their main cooking oil but, as the trees grow haphazardly in arid soil, requiring little maintenance and providing fodder for goats, its production may increase if modern methods are introduced. From the residue of the pressed oil, the village women also make a paste called *amlou*, which is sweetened with honey and bound with ground almonds. This thick nutty paste is served with bread at breakfast, or for a snack. Sitting around a warm stove, stoked by the women with the bark and nut shells of the argan tree, drinking saffron tea with freshly baked flat bread dipped in *amlou*, it is comforting to think that these rural people could have a wealthier future if their golden nectar attracts the same passion as its olive cousin.

roasted courgette and apple salad with oranges
slada gharaa bil tofah

The courgette is a popular summer vegetable in Morocco and, as it marries well with fresh herbs and garlic, it appears frequently in salads and dips as well as in vegetable and meat tagines. Served as a starter or as an accompaniment to a meat and poultry dish, this salad is delightfully refreshing.

2 medium courgettes, trimmed, cut in half crossways and sliced lengthways

1 green apple, cored, cut in half lengthways and sliced crossways

3 tablespoons olive oil

freshly squeezed juice of 1 lemon

1 tablespoon runny honey

2 sweet oranges, peeled with pith removed

rind of ½ preserved lemon, finely shredded (see page 11)

a small bunch of fresh mint leaves, shredded

sea salt

Serves 4–6

Preheat the oven to 200°C (400°F) Gas 6. Put the sliced courgette and apple in a baking dish and spoon over the oil. Pop them in the oven for about 20 minutes. Take them out of the oven and pour over the lemon juice and honey. Pop them back into the oven for a further 10 minutes, until they have softened and are slightly golden in colour. Leave them to cool in the dish.

Prepare the oranges on a plate to catch the juice. Slice them thinly into neat circles, remove any pips and arrange them on a serving dish. Spoon the roasted courgette and apple on top of the oranges. Stir the orange juice that you have caught on the plate into the roasting juices in the baking dish and season with a little salt. Drizzle the juice over the salad and scatter the preserved lemon and mint over the top. Serve chilled or at room temperature.

green olive salad with bitter orange peel
zaytoun meslalla

The most ubiquitous snack or *kemia* dish is a bowl of plump, juicy olives, gleaming in their olive oil coating and looking resplendent in their varying shades of black, violet, reddish-brown and green. Olives also play a principal role in a number of tagines, dips and salads, such as this one which is generally served on its own with chunks of warm, crusty bread to dip into it. The peel of fresh, or preserved, bitter oranges are used for this dish but if you have difficulty finding bitter oranges, substitute the peel with that of half a preserved lemon.

350 g fleshy green olives, stoned and cut into slivers

1–2 teaspoons coriander seeds, roasted and crushed

peel of ½ bitter orange, finely chopped or sliced

3 tablespoons olive oil

flat or leavened bread, for dipping

Serves 3–4

Tip the olives into a bowl and stir in the coriander seeds and bitter orange peel. Bind with the olive oil, cover and leave to sit for an hour before serving. (You can also make this ahead of time and store it in a sealed container in the refrigerator for 2–3 days). Serve with warm chunks of flat, or leavened, bread to dip in it.

chickpea salad with onions and paprika
slada hummas

Chickpeas, beans and lentils are consumed daily in rural Morocco, particularly in areas where meat is scarce or expensive. They are cooked in stews, added to couscous, and find their way into salads. This dish is particularly good served warm and is often topped with crumbled goats' cheese from the village.

225 g dried chickpeas, soaked in plenty of cold water overnight

1 red onion, cut in half lengthways, then in half crossways, and sliced with the grain

4 garlic cloves, finely chopped

1 teaspoon ground cumin

1–2 teaspoons paprika

3 tablespoons olive oil

freshly squeezed juice of 1 lemon

a small bunch of fresh flat leaf parsley, coarsely chopped

a small bunch of fresh coriander, coarsely chopped

125 g goats' cheese, or feta, crumbled (optional)

sea salt and freshly ground black pepper

bread, to serve

Serves 4

Drain the chickpeas and put them in a deep pan. Cover with water and bring to the boil. Reduce the heat and simmer for about 45 minutes, until the chickpeas are tender but not mushy. Drain the chickpeas and remove any loose skins – you can rub them in a clean tea towel to remove them, or between your fingers.

Tip the warm chickpeas into a bowl. Add the onion, garlic, cumin and paprika and toss in the olive oil and lemon juice while the chickpeas are still warm, making sure they are all well coated. Season with salt and pepper to taste and toss in most of the herbs. Crumble over the goats' cheese, if using, and sprinkle with the rest of the herbs. Serve while still warm with bread.

pear and chicory salad with rose petals
slada bouawid

Moroccans love to scatter rose petals in salads, over tablecloths and in the small fountains of medinas and riads. Most gardens and courtyards boast several scented rose bushes among the pots of herbs. In this delightfully pretty salad, the sweetness of the pear balances the bitterness of the chicory leaves and both are enhanced by the perfume and floral taste of rose petals.

2–3 ripe, but firm, pears, cut into 8 segments and cored

2 white, or pink, chicory, trimmed and leaves separated

2–3 tablespoons olive or argan oil

freshly squeezed juice of ½ lemon

2 teaspoons honey

sea salt and freshly ground black pepper

a handful of fresh, scented rose petals

Serves 4–6

Arrange the pear segments and chicory leaves in a shallow serving bowl. Mix together the oil, lemon juice and honey and season to taste with salt and pepper. Pour the mixture over the salad. Scatter the rose petals over the top and only toss the salad when ready to serve, otherwise the petals become soggy.

soups, breads and savoury pastries

rustic tomato and vegetable soup with *ras-el-hanout*
chorba b'hodra

3 tablespoons olive oil with a small knob of butter, or 3 tablespoons ghee

2 onions, chopped

1 butternut squash, peeled, deseeded and cut into small chunks

4 celery stalks, chopped

2 carrots, peeled and chopped

1–2 teaspoons ground turmeric

2–3 teaspoons Ras-el-hanout *(see page 93)*

1 tablespoon sugar

800 g tinned chopped tomatoes, drained of juice

1 tablespoon tomato purée

1.5 litres vegetable or chicken stock

4–5 tablespoons full-fat natural yoghurt

a bunch of fresh coriander leaves, roughly chopped

sea salt and freshly ground black pepper

bread, to serve

Serves 4–6

The thick vegetable soups prepared daily in most homes are known as *chorba*. Often they will suffice as a meal on their own with bread, or they may be served as a starter. Chunky and spicy, this is a rustic *chorba* which, served with a cooling dollop of creamy yoghurt, is extremely tasty and satisfying.

Heat the oil and butter in a deep heavy-based saucepan and stir in the onions, squash, celery and carrots. Cook for 4–5 minutes, until the vegetables begin to soften and take on a little colour. Stir in the turmeric, ras-el-hanout, and sugar, then add the tomatoes. Stir in the tomato purée and pour in the stock. Bring the liquid to the boil, reduce the heat and simmer for 30–40 minutes, until the vegetables are very tender and the liquid has reduced a little.

Season the soup to taste with salt and pepper and ladle it into warm serving bowls. Swirl a spoonful of yoghurt on the top of each serving and sprinkle with the chopped coriander. Serve immediately with chunks of warm, crusty bread.

Islam, Ramadan and bread

After the invasion by the Arabs between the seventh and fourteenth centuries, the majority of Moroccans adopted Islam and its inherent restrictions regarding certain foods and the consumption of alcohol. Muslim by faith, but aware of their diverse cultural identities, they live in harmony with the Moroccan Jews who share many of the same culinary beliefs, such as the importance of hospitality and the sharing of bread, which is regarded as sacred in both religions. The religious laws may differ, but the festivities and feasting take place in a similar fashion. As the Prophet Mohammed proclaimed all food to be sacred, some dishes are invested with particular religious significance. The best known of these is *harira*, a thick, hearty soup packed with vegetables and pulses that is served to break the fast during Ramadan. In traditional Berber households, *harira* is eaten from earthenware bowls using rounded spoons carved from lemon wood. The soup is served with either a sweet bread, or the traditional, partially leavened, daily loaf, *khubz*. Handfuls of dates are also eaten to break the fast, before tucking into an array of tangy salads, delectable tagines and couscous.

Ramadan is the ninth month of the Muslim calendar, commemorating the time when the Koran was revealed to the Prophet. For the Moroccan Muslims, this means a month of fasting from dawn to sunset and this includes drinking and smoking. It is therefore a time of reflection and purification and, for some, a real endurance test. Once the sun sets though, there are smiles on faces and the streets become alive with culinary activity. Street food is at its best during Ramadan as special breads and sweet pastries are sold everywhere – in the markets and squares, at bus stations and taxi ranks. The aroma of roasted meat and grilled *kefta* waft around every corner of the souks, and cauldrons of *harira* are prepared at makeshift stalls. With the first sighting of the moon at the end of the month, a new celebration begins. This is Aid el Fitr which marks the end of Ramadan and the beginning of the month of Choual. It is a time of joy as families celebrate with a great deal of feasting. People visit each other bearing gifts of sweets and sweet pastries and it is traditional to give dates, grain and money to the poor.

Two lunar months after Aid el Fitr comes another religious event, Eid el Kebir. This is the Islamic celebration of the Angel Gabriel's descent from heaven to prevent Ibrahim (Abraham) from sacrificing his son, Ismail (Isaac). Instead, Ibrahim sacrifices a ram, which has led to the tradition in Muslim communities for the head of a family to slaughter a ram to mark the event. The festivities can last for as long as a week, as banks and businesses close and people go back to their villages, or to their families in other cities. The sight of rams being carried around on shoulders, led through the streets by a rope, stuffed into the boot of a car, or draped over a moped, is almost comical but very real, as every family purchases one, takes it home to feed and then slaughters it in a ritual manner. First the ram is made to face East, towards Mecca, then the throat is cut swiftly with the sharp blade of knife. The animal is then skilfully fleeced and divided into joints of various importance – the head is prized for steaming and will be served to a guest, or the most important member of the household; the ram's testes and penis are generally grilled and regarded as an honour to eat; the hind legs are roasted, and the cuts in between end up in various soups and tagines, and some get minced for *kefta*. The whole affair is one of industry and merriment as the men carry out the butchering while the women focus on the cooking.

Other festive occasions with religious significance in Morocco include Mouharram, the first day of the lunar New Year and the day of the Hijra, the migration of the Prophet Mohammed from Mecca to Medina. Another day to donate to the poor is Aid el Achoura, the tenth day of the first month, when everyone must give one-tenth of everything one has to the poor. The day is usually celebrated with a huge dish of couscous and chicken. The birthday of the Prophet Mohammed is marked by a religious holiday, El Mawlid Ennabaoui, when everything closes and the sacks of couscous suddenly vanish from the markets as families rush home to prepare and eat great mounds of it as it is a gift from Allah.

Throughout the Islamic world, bread is sacred and should never be wasted. Moroccans will rescue bread lying in the street, or left unfinished on a table and give it to the poor, to pets or to livestock. Bread that is found will be picked up, held to the forehead and kissed, giving thanks to Allah, and a cook will bless the flour, water and yeast before making the bread dough. Daily loaves are usually simple, half leavened, rustic-looking breads which are broken with the right hand when ready to eat, or cut into portions before being brought to the table. As the custom is to eat from a communal dish, bread is in essence a piece of useful, edible cutlery, as small pieces held between the thumb and first two fingers are dipped into sauces, soups and puréed salads, or employed as a scoop for juicy morsels and chunks of meat.

Very few Moroccan households possess an oven, so almost every neighbourhood, or village, shares a communal oven where the bread and pastries are baked and large cuts of meat can be roasted. In the countryside the traditional oven is made of mud, similar to a clay tandoori oven, and the loaves are often handcrafted into particular shapes and designs to identify them from others. There is a variety of traditional Moroccan breads but the most common are flat breads, semolina buns and baguette-style loaves, a legacy of the French. For Moroccans, a meal without bread, just like couscous, would be unthinkable.

Variations of this soup can be found throughout the Islamic world. In Morocco alone there are at least a dozen versions, differentiated by their regional recipes and by the pulses and vegetables used in the soup. It is one of the classic dishes prepared at religious feasts and it is traditionally served to break the fast during Ramadan, the month of fasting. Thick and hearty, with a consistency that comes somewhere between a soup and a stew, it can be served as a meal on its own with thick, crusty bread, flat bread or with rustic semolina rolls.

classic lamb, chickpea and lentil soup with cumin
harira

2–3 tablespoons olive or argan oil

2 onions, chopped

2 celery stalks, diced

2 small carrots, peeled and diced

2–3 garlic cloves, left whole and smashed

1 tablespoon cumin seeds

450 g lean lamb, cut into bite-sized cubes

2–3 teaspoons ground turmeric

2 teaspoons paprika

2 teaspoons ground cinnamon

2 teaspoons sugar

2 bay leaves

2 tablespoons tomato purée

1 litre lamb or chicken stock

1 x 400 g tin of chickpeas, drained and rinsed

1 x 400 g tin of chopped tomatoes, drained of juice

100 g brown or green lentils, rinsed

a small bunch of fresh flat leaf parsley, coarsely chopped

a small bunch of fresh coriander, coarsely chopped

sea salt and freshly ground black pepper

1 lemon, cut into quarters, to garnish

Serves 4–6

Heat the oil in a deep, heavy-based saucepan. Stir in the onions, celery and carrots and cook until the onions begin to colour. Add the smashed garlic and cumin seeds and toss in the lamb. Cook until lightly browned. Add the spices, sugar and bay leaves and stir in the tomato purée. Pour in the stock and bring the liquid to the boil. Reduce the heat, cover with a lid, and simmer for 1 hour, until the meat is tender.

Add the chopped tomatoes, chickpeas and lentils to the pan and cook gently for a further 30 minutes, until the lentils are soft and the soup is almost as thick as a stew. Top up with a little water, if necessary, as the lentils will absorb most of it. Season the soup with salt and pepper and add most of the parsley and coriander.

Serve the soupy stew piping hot, sprinkled with the remaining parsley and coriander and with wedges of lemon to squeeze over it and plenty of bread for dipping.

fish soup with lemon and harissa
chorba bil hout

2–3 tablespoons olive oil

1 onion, finely chopped.

2 celery stalks, diced

2–3 garlic cloves, finely chopped

1–2 teaspoons Harissa (see page 11)

a small bunch of fresh flat leaf parsley, finely chopped

1 litre fish stock or water

freshly squeezed juice of 2 lemons

1 glass fino sherry or white wine (optional)

1 x 400 g tin of chopped tomatoes, drained of juice

1 kg firm-fleshed fish, such as cod, haddock, ling, grouper, sea bass or snapper, cut into large chunks

500 g shellfish, such as prawns, clams and mussels, cleaned and in their shells

a small bunch of fresh coriander leaves, coarsely chopped

sea salt and freshly ground black pepper

bread or couscous, to serve

Serves 4–6

Although Morocco boasts an extensive coastline, there are few fish soups on the national menu as the bulk of the daily catch is grilled in the streets, baked with dates or olives or simmered with herbs and spices in tagines. However, in some of the northern coastal areas, such as Casablanca, Tangier and Tetouan, there are a few gems that echo the well-flavoured soupy stews of Mediterranean Spain and France. Soups of this nature are often best served on their own with plenty of crusty bread, or spooned over plain couscous.

Heat the oil in a deep, heavy based saucepan, stir in the onion, celery and garlic and fry gently until it begins to colour. Add the harissa and parsley and pour in the stock. Bring the liquid to the boil, reduce the heat and simmer gently for 10 minutes to allow the flavours to mingle.

Add the lemon juice and fino sherry, if using, and stir in the tomatoes. Season to taste with salt and pepper. Gently stir in the fish chunks and shellfish and bring the liquid to the boil again. Reduce the heat and simmer for 3–4 minutes, until the fish is cooked through. Sprinkle the chopped coriander over the top and serve immediately with lots of bread or couscous.

creamy pumpkin soup with aniseed and saffron
crème de potiron

This is a lovely, nourishing and very moreish pumpkin soup from Casablanca. It includes the warm flavours of aniseed and cloves, which are believed to aid digestion, and a hint of floral notes from the saffron, which enhances the overall pleasure of this delicate soup as well as its vibrant colour. It is best served on its own as a starter.

500 g pumpkin flesh, peeled, deseeded and cubed

1 celery stalk, cut into 4 pieces

3–4 cloves

2 onions, peeled and left whole

1 bay leaf

1 tablespoon aniseeds, tied up in a piece of muslin

1–2 teaspoons saffron fronds

1.25 litres milk

100 g butter, ghee or smen

a small bunch of fresh flat leaf parsley, finely chopped

sea salt and freshly ground black pepper

Serves 4

Put the pumpkin flesh and celery in a heavy-based saucepan. Stick the cloves into the onions and add them to the pan, along with the bay leaf, the muslin bag of aniseeds and the saffron fronds. Pour in the milk and heat gently until it reaches scalding point. Reduce the heat, partially cover and simmer gently for about 45 minutes, until the pumpkin is soft.

Remove and discard the celery, onions, bay leaf and the muslin bag of aniseeds and saffron. Pour the soup into a blender and whizz until smooth. Pour it into a clean pan and beat in the butter, bit by bit, until it has melted. Season the soup to taste with salt and pepper and heat over medium heat, until it reaches scalding point again. Ladle the soup into warm serving bowls, sprinkle with parsley and serve immediately.

As most dishes are eaten with hands rather than cutlery, the first stage of any meal involves the passing around of the bread which is used to scoop, mop or shovel food from the serving dish to the mouth. Bread is a vital component of every meal and is regarded as sacred. Like couscous, bread varies from region to region and is baked in households and villages every day. A common Berber breakfast consists of freshly baked bread dipped in the local fruity olive oil. For ceremonial occasions, aniseed or fennel seeds are often used to flavour the bread dough, which can be shaped into loaves or rolls.

Moroccan country bread
kesra

½ teaspoon dried yeast

1 teaspoon sugar

450 g unbleached white flour

75 g cornmeal (reserve 1 tablespoon for dusting)

1 teaspoon salt

2 tablespoons melted butter or ghee

500 ml lukewarm water

sesame seeds, for sprinkling

2 baking trays

Makes 2 loaves

Put the yeast and sugar in a small bowl with about 60 ml water. Sift the flour, cornmeal and salt into a large bowl. Make a well in the centre and pour in the dissolved yeast mixture and melted butter. Gradually add the lukewarm water, using your hands to draw in the flour from the sides to form the mixture into a dough. Add more flour if the dough gets too sticky.

Turn the dough out on to a floured surface and knead it until it becomes smooth and elastic. Divide the dough into 2 pieces. Knead each piece into a ball, then flatten and stretch them into circles, roughly 20 cm in diameter. Lightly oil 2 baking trays and dust them with the reserved cornmeal. Place 1 round of dough on each baking tray and sprinkle with sesame seeds. Cover them with a damp cloth and leave them in a warm place for about 1 hour, until they have doubled in size.

Preheat the oven to 220°C (425°F) Gas 7. Pinch the top of each loaf with your fingers, or prick them with a fork. Pop them into the preheated oven and bake for 15 minutes, then reduce the heat to 180°C (350°F) Gas 4 and bake for a further 15 minutes, until the loaves are crusty and golden and sound hollow when tapped on the bottom.

A variety of loaves of different shapes and sizes are baked for both Jewish and Muslim festive occasions. Spiced buns and plaited loaves are particularly festive, enjoyed for breakfast and throughout the day with soup and tagines.

spiced festive bread
chollo

25 g fresh yeast
225 ml lukewarm water
2–3 teaspoons sugar
450 g strong plain flour
1 teaspoon salt
1 teaspoon aniseeds
2 teaspoons sesame seeds
50 ml sunflower or olive oil
1 egg, lightly beaten

For glazing:
1 egg, beaten
50 ml whole milk
1 teaspoon sesame seeds

a baking tray

Makes 2 loaves

Cream the yeast in a small bowl with 50 ml of the lukewarm water and 1 teaspoon of the sugar, until it dissolves and becomes frothy.

Sift the flour and salt into a large bowl and stir in the aniseeds and sesame seeds. Make a well in the centre of the flour and add the yeast mixture, oil, egg and the rest of the sugar. Pour in the remaining lukewarm water, using your hands to draw in the flour from the sides to form a smooth dough.

Take the dough out of the bowl and knead it on a lightly floured surface for about 10 minutes until it becomes light and elastic. Divide the dough into 2 balls and divide each ball into 3. Knead and stretch the first 3 into ropes about 30 cm long. Line the ropes side by side and plait them together. Pinch the ends together. Repeat with the other 3 balls of dough to form a second loaf.

Place the 2 plaited loaves on a floured baking tray. Cover them with a damp tea towel and leave them in a warm place for about 1 hour, until they have doubled in size.

Preheat the oven to 180°C (350°F) Gas 4. To make the glaze, put the egg and milk in a bowl and beat well. Brush it over the loaves. Sprinkle the tops with sesame seeds and bake them in the preheated oven for about 40 minutes, until the loaves sound hollow when you tap them on the base. Transfer to a wire rack to cool a little, then serve with jam, honey or as an accompaniment to savoury dishes.

dadas and the traditional kitchen

Until recently, cooking in Morocco was solely a woman's art; the kitchen her domain. Recipes were not written down but passed orally from generation to generation. In a man's world, the kitchen was a very feminine place – a place for gossip, for healing, for bonding – and cooking was regarded as a woman's gift from God. Men rarely entered this private culinary zone. Much of this rings true today but in some of the more cosmopolitan cities there is a growing number of male kitchen apprentices and several well-known male chefs.

One of Morocco's culinary secrets is the tradition of the dadas, women of African origin, descended from slaves who were brought into the country from the Sudan and parts of central Africa. Once the hidden face of Morocco, dadas were purchased by wealthy Arab and Berber households to cook for them. Shrouded in mystique, they were kept in a form of bondage within the vicinity of the kitchen and remained illiterate. In the cities of Fes, Meknes and Marrakesh, the men of wealthy households often acquired a young dada as a third or fourth wife. If this wife bore any children, or if the dada of a household bore illegitimate children, they would usually be brought up in the household and the female offspring would enter the realm of the dadas and carry on the tradition.

Nowadays, there is a law that protects young girls from working in households and, although the dada tradition survives, the women themselves have become emancipated and run kitchens in prestigious restaurants and hotels, or work for catering companies that hire them out to wealthy families to prepare the *diffas* – the large feasts to celebrate special occasions, such as weddings. The catering company itself will usually be headed by a man, as business is still a man's domain, and he will make all the arrangements with the family, while the dadas dwell behind the scenes in the kitchens for several days, purchasing all the food from the markets, slaughtering the sheep, preparing the *warka* for the savoury and sweet pastries, and squatting on the floor, preparing ingredients using traditional Maghrebi kitchen tools.

The traditional dada was, and still is, the 'priestess' of the kitchen. Dressed in robes and a turban, the long sleeves tied around the wrists with a silk cord, and bangles jangling around her wrists and ankles, creating a mystical tinkle from the depths of the dark, spartan kitchen. Even in the grandest of riads, the kitchen is the most basic room in the house, cool in the summer but damp in the winter months. The cooking utensils are simple, consisting of glazed earthenware tagines and copper pots for cooking, wooden spoons and a mortar and pestle, or grinding stone, for spices. There will be a portable, charcoal-fed *kanoun*, a small clay stove on which the tagines sit and which lends its flavour to the grilled *kefta* and fish cooked over it. In some wealthy households, there may be a larger stove for baking and roasting too, otherwise the neighbourhood communal oven is used. A *keskess*, a colander capped pot, is used for making couscous; a shallow earthenware platter, a *ga'saa* is used for kneading dough or for rolling the semolina to make the couscous; and a folded carpet is placed on the floor to serve as a seat.

At first glance all the grandeur, colour and exoticism of the cooked dishes seems absent in the kitchen, until it comes to life in the presence of a dada, or the women of the household, as they skillfully prepare a feast. Allah's blessing may be called upon before the cooking commences, incense is often thrown into the fire to drive away the devil, *jnoun*, and like a magician's cave, the darkness is suddenly illuminated with warmth and industry as the sound of the pounding pestle begins, while the air fills with whiffs of freshly chopped coriander and parsley and the aroma of garlic, onions and cumin toasting in olive oil, punctuated by subtle hints of saffron, rose petals and orange blossom.

I was lucky enough to meet the lovely dada, Laaziza Grizmi, the queen of the kitchen at La Maison Arabe in Marrakesh. Unaware of her African ancestry and quite clear that her father had been Berber, she is the epitome of a traditional dada. Dressed in her white robe, with a cherubic, kind and ageless face, she is shy in company, but a wizard in the kitchen. Obviously the skills and elusive magic wielded by the dadas, passed down from mother to daughter, had taken hold of Laaziza but the stories of slavery and ancestry seem to have blown away with the desert wind. Running the kitchen in one of the best restaurants in Marrakesh can be no easy task but, in addition to that, she leads cookery workshops for enthusiasts from all over the world, even though she only speaks Arabic. Food, fortunately, has a language of its own and cooking runs through Laaziza's veins. She learnt from her mother, but she smiles at the thought of her own daughter who is not interested in cooking at all. In Laaziza's youth, if you were a girl, you inherited the dada mantle. When asked if she thinks the dada tradition is dying out, Laaziza smiles the sweetest of knowing smiles. It is possible, she answers, as there are many choices for young girls and they no longer want to cook. When girls get married, they want to go out to eat so, of course, young men will enter the domain and change the face of Morocco's culinary culture.

classic chicken pie with cinnamon
b'stilla b'djej

This is a homely version of the traditional *b'stilla*, an elaborate pie made with pigeon or squab, which is prepared for special occasions such as weddings. Thought to be of Andalusian origin, this magnificent pie should be sampled at least once on any visit to Morocco. Wafer thin sheets of the local dough, *ouarka*, are used for this dish, but ready-made filo works well as a substitute.

2–3 tablespoons olive oil

100 g butter

3 onions, cut in half lengthways, then in half crossways and sliced with the grain

2 garlic cloves, chopped

2–3 tablespoons blanched almonds, chopped

1–2 teaspoons ground cinnamon plus 1–2 teaspoons for dusting

1 teaspoon ground ginger

1 teaspoon paprika

1 teaspoon ground coriander

250 g chicken fillets, cut into bite-sized pieces

a bunch of fresh flat leaf parsley, finely chopped

a bunch of fresh coriander, finely chopped

7–8 sheets filo pastry

1 egg yolk

2–3 teaspoons icing sugar, for dusting

sea salt and freshly ground black pepper

a large round, ovenproof dish

Serves 4–6

Preheat the oven to 200°C (400°F) Gas 6. In a heavy-based frying pan, heat the olive oil with a nut of the butter and stir in the onions. Fry over medium heat for 5–6 minutes, until they begin to soften and colour. Stir in the garlic and almonds and fry until they begin to colour. Add the spices, toss in the chicken and cook gently, until all the liquid in the pan has evaporated. Toss in the herbs and season with salt and pepper. Remove the pan from the heat and leave to cool.

Melt the rest of butter. Separate the sheets of filo and cover them with a damp cloth. Brush a little butter over the base of the ovenproof dish and cover with a sheet of filo, allowing the sides to flop over the edge. Brush with butter and place another one on top. Repeat with another 2 layers. Spread the chicken and onion mixture on top of the filo and fold the edges over the filling. Cover with the remaining sheets of filo, brushing each one with butter before adding the next. Tuck the overlapping edges under the pie, like making a bed, so that it is flat on top. Mix the egg yolk with ½ teaspoon water and brush it over the top of the pie.

Bake in the preheated oven for about 25 minutes, until the pastry is crisp and golden. Dust the top with the icing sugar and cinnamon in a lattice pattern and serve immediately.

savoury pastries filled with spicy minced meat
briouats

1–2 tablespoons olive oil

1 onion, finely chopped

2 tablespoons blanched almonds, chopped

1 teaspoon Ras-el-Hanout (see page 93)

225 g finely minced beef

8 sheets filo pastry

sunflower oil, for deep-frying

salt and freshly ground black pepper

Serves 4–6

Briouats are little savoury pastries that can be filled with a variety of ingredients, such as saffron-flavoured chicken, spinach or spicy minced lamb or beef. Popular as street food, or as hot starters, *briouats* are as familiar a sight as kebabs or brochettes.

Heat the oil in a heavy-based pan and stir in the onion and the chopped almonds. Just as they begin to colour, stir in the ras-el-hanout. Add the minced beef and cook until well browned and cooked through. Season to taste with salt and pepper and let cool.

Lay the sheets of filo on a flat surface, cut them into strips about 8–10 cm wide and cover them with a damp cloth. Take a strip and spoon a little of the filling mixture on the short end nearest to you. Fold the corners over the mixture to seal it, then roll it away from you into a tight cigar shape. As you reach the end of the strip, brush it with a little water and continue to roll. Repeat with the remaining strips and filling. Keep the pastries covered with a damp cloth to prevent them from drying out before you are ready to cook them.

Heat sufficient sunflower oil for deep-frying in a saucepan and fry the cigars over a medium heat, until golden brown. Drain on kitchen paper and serve warm.

pastry triangles filled with tuna and egg
brik

Popular street food in the coastal areas, these tuna and egg-filled pastries are originally from neighbouring Tunisia, but have been adopted by the Moroccans. As the egg is designed to be runny inside the pastry, there is an art to eating them by holding the corners of the pastry as you bite into the middle.

Heat the oil in a frying pan and stir in the onions for 2 minutes to soften them. Add the anchovies and fry gently until they melt into the oil. Turn off the heat and leave the mixture to cool. Tip the cooked onion mixture into a bowl and add the tuna. Break up the tuna with a fork and add the capers and parsley. Mix well to combine.

Place the filo squares on a work surface and spoon one quarter of the mixture onto one half of a square in the shape of a triangle. Make a well in the tuna mixture and crack an egg into it. Fold the empty side of the filo over the filling, taking care not to move or break the yolk of the egg, and then seal the edges with a little water. Repeat with the 3 other pastry squares.

Heat sufficient oil for shallow frying in a heavy-based frying pan and slip one of the pastries into the oil. Fry for less than 1 minute on each side. When crisp and golden brown, carefully lift the pastry out of the pan using a slotted spoon and drain it on kitchen paper. Repeat with the other pastries and serve warm while the yolk is still runny.

1 tablespoon olive oil

1 onion, finely chopped

6–8 anchovy fillets

1 x 200 g tin of tuna, drained

1 tablespoon capers, rinsed and drained

a small bunch fresh flat leaf parsley, finely chopped

2 sheets filo pastry, cut into 20 cm squares

4 eggs

sunflower oil, for shallow frying

Serves 4

baked pastries with seafood
rghaif

15 g fresh yeast

400 ml lukewarm water

350 g plain flour

1 teaspoon salt

175 ml sunflower oil

sunflower oil, for working the dough

1 egg yolk mixed with 1 tablespoon water, for brushing

For the filling:

freshly squeezed juice of 3 lemons

175 g small fresh prawns, shelled and deveined

175 g small squid, with ink sack, back bone and head removed, and thinly sliced

2–3 tablespoons olive oil and a nut of butter

2 onions, finely chopped

2 garlic cloves, crushed

1 red or green chilli, deseeded and finely chopped

1 teaspoon ground cumin

1 teaspoon ground coriander

1 teaspoon paprika

a bunch of fresh coriander, finely chopped

a bunch of fresh flat leaf parsley, finely chopped

sea salt and freshly ground black pepper

a baking tray, lightly oiled

Serves 4–6

This is a delicious seafood pastry which can be adapted to encase a chicken and saffron filling, or vegetables with cheese. You can watch these pastries being assembled in front of you at some of the seafront restaurants in the pretty blue and white coastal town, Essaouira, where they are cooked on makeshift griddles. At home, you can use a griddle or bake them in the oven.

In a small bowl, cream the yeast with roughly 100 ml of the warm water and leave it in a warm place until frothy.

Sift the flour and the salt into a wide-rimmed bowl and make a well in the centre. Pour the oil and the yeast mixture into the well. Gradually, add the remaining water as you draw the flour in from the sides of the bowl and knead the mixture with your hands to form a smooth, soft dough. Divide the dough into 12 equal balls, place them on a lightly oiled surface and cover with a damp tea towel. Leave to prove for about 1 hour, until they have doubled in size.

Meanwhile, prepare the filling. Bring a pan of water and half the lemon juice to the boil. Drop in the prawns and squid, cook for 2–3 minutes then drain and refresh under cold running water. Set aside.

Heat the olive oil and butter in a heavy-based pan and stir in the onions, garlic and chilli. Cook for for 2–3 minutes, until they begin to colour. Stir in the spices and toss in the cooked prawns and squid. Add the herbs and the rest of the lemon juice and season to taste with salt and pepper. Turn off the heat and leave the mixture to cool.

Preheat the oven to 180°C (350°F) Gas 4. Take a ball of dough, put it on a lightly oiled surface, then spread and stretch it with your fingers to form a thin circle about 12–15 cm diameter. Repeat with the remaining balls of dough. Put a large spoonful of the seafood mixture just off centre in each circle. Fold the narrower edge over the mixture, tuck in the ends, then fold the wider edge over to seal in the mixture and form a square package. Place the pastries sealed-side down on an oiled baking tray and brush them with a little of the egg yolk mixture. Bake the pastries for about 30 minutes, until golden, and eat immediately as a snack, or as a course on its own.

tagines, *k'dras* and couscous

Berber traditions and tagines

The root of Moroccan cooking can be traced back to the indigenous Berber tribes. Steeped in tradition, the rural Berbers are proud of their ancestry. They have lived in North Africa, between Egypt and the western coast of Morocco, as far back as archaeological records go. Originally farmers, living alongside the nomadic Taureg and Bedouin of the desert, the Berbers would have made an impact on the food of the region long before the invasion of the Arabs and, although they had to convert from Christianity to Islam and adopt new religious and culinary customs, they are keen to make the point that they are not of Arab descent. Many rural Berber communities speak their own languages and dialects but those who are literate also speak Arabic and, in some areas, French. Berbers also fiercely uphold some of their own culinary customs, such as the festive pilgrimages, *moussems*, which are held in tented enclosures where traditional dishes, such as couscous, are cooked in vast quantities and shared. Another feature of Berber culinary life is the *diffa*, which is a festive banquet, varying in content in accordance with the wealth of the family, to mark special occasions such as weddings, births, circumcisions and religious events. One of the traditional Berber dishes cooked at a *diffa* is *mechoui*, which involves rubbing a whole lamb or kid with a spice paste consisting mainly of cumin, black pepper and garlic blended with *smen*, the rancid tasting butter, and slow-roasting it on a spit over embers set in a deep pit in the ground. The lamb is cooked for 5–6 hours and basted frequently to give a moist, tender and flavoursome meat. The cooking process is carried out by the men and is followed by feasting that may last several days.

The traditional dishes of the mountain and desert Berbers are basic and rustic, almost as if the cuisines of the royal dynasties simply passed them by. An example of this simplicity is the Berber speciality *tangia*, which consists of meat cooked in an earthenware amphora-shaped vessel. Like *mechoui* this is one of the few dishes prepared by the men of a village or neighbourhood. The Marrakesh version, Marrakchi *tangia* is reputed to be the most succulent. The lamb, which is flavoured with saffron and preserved lemon, is sealed in the amphora with parchment paper that is tied with string and is cooked very slowly in the embers of a fire. The resulting texture of the meat is so tender it literally melts in the mouth like butter with a delicate aromatic taste that is divine.

We also have the Berbers to thank for tagines and couscous. A predominant feature of Moroccan cuisine, the tagine is a slow-cooked stew, deeply aromatic and full of flavour. The word 'tagine' (*tajine* in Arabic) is the name of the cooked dish as well as the traditional, earthenware cooking vessel, a *tajine slaoui*, with its majestic conical lid. Placed over a charcoal stove, a *kanoun*, which is constantly replenished with embers and disperses the heat all around the base, the *tajine slaoui* enables the ingredients to cook gently so that they remain beautifully tender and moist in a reduced sauce that sizzles in its own fat. In rural areas, you will often come across tagines lined up regimentally by the side of a road, or at the edge of a country restaurant. The enticing aroma of cooking spices will inevitably draw you in and you will be offered the 'tagine of the day', which could be lamb with artichokes and peas, beef with aubergines and dates, duck with quince and walnuts, meat balls with mint and lemon, or the most traditional of them all, lamb with prunes, apricots and honey.

Many of the traditional tagines are distinguished by their cooking fats and spices. The *tfaia* tagines are prepared with *smen* and served with almonds and boiled eggs; *qamama* tagines are made with lots of onions, honey and lemon and are fairly pungent; *m'quali* tagines are flavoured with saffron and ginger. For large numbers of people it is not possible to use the *tajine slaoui*, as they are not big enough, so large tin-lined copper or aluminium pots called *k'dras* are used instead. The trademark of a *k'dra* is that the ingredients are cooked in *smen*.

The method employed in tagine cooking also varies from the countryside to the cities. In the north, in cities like Tangier and Casablanca, where the Spanish and French influences are evident, the meat is often browned in butter or oil and the spices and onions are sautéed before adding the rest of the ingredients, whereas Fassi and Marrakchi tagines are often prepared by putting all the ingredients together in water and then adding extra butter or *smen* towards the end. Tagines can be served from the cooking vessels, or transferred to an ornate serving tagine, decorated with pretty blue, turquoise, green, yellow and red patterns, which enhance the overall pleasure when serving to guests.

When it comes to buying a tagine, there are several different types and sizes choose from, as some represent a Berber tribe, a particular village or a region of Morocco. To be used for cooking, they must be glazed and treated by soaking them in water for 24 hours. Some also benefit from being seasoned by placing bay leaves and dried sage in the base along with a roughly chopped onion, garlic and a generous dollop of olive oil, then filled with water and very gently heated through – this removes the earthenware taste from the base and prepares it for prolonged cooking over heat. However, none of them will last for long on conventional hobs without the aid of a diffuser and, even then, some develop tiny cracks that render them useless. The answer is to buy the charcoal stove too, or to invest in the fool-proof tagine sold by Le Creuset. This version looks just like a beautifully glazed tagine with an earthenware conical lid, but the base is cast iron enabling it to be used on gas or electric hobs.

classic lamb tagine with almonds, prunes and apricots
tajine bil barkok wal loz

1–2 tablespoons olive oil

2 tablespoons blanched almonds

2 red onions, finely chopped

2–3 garlic cloves, finely chopped

a thumb-sized piece of fresh ginger, peeled and chopped

a pinch of saffron fronds

2 cinnamon sticks

1–2 teaspoons coriander seeds, crushed

500 g boned lamb, from the shoulder, leg or shanks, trimmed and cubed

about 12 stoned prunes and 6 dried apricots, soaked in cold water for 1 hour and drained

3–4 strips orange rind

1–2 tablespoons dark honey

a handful of fresh coriander leaves, chopped

sea salt and freshly ground black pepper

bread or Plain, Buttery Couscous (see page 77), to serve

Serves 4–6

This is perhaps the best known of all Moroccan tagines. Aromatic, sweet, succulent and juicy with the addition of the fruit, this is a perfect introduction to the tastes of Morocco. Traditionally this dish would be served with bread to mop up the syrupy sauce, or you can serve it with couscous.

Heat the oil in the base of a tagine or a heavy-based casserole. Add the almonds and cook, stirring, until they turn golden. Add the onions and garlic and sauté until they begin to colour. Stir in the ginger, saffron, cinnamon sticks and coriander seeds. Toss the lamb into the tagine and sauté for 1–2 minutes, stirring to make sure it is coated in the onion and spices .

Pour in enough water to just cover the meat then bring it to the boil. Reduce the heat, put the lid on the tagine and simmer for 1 hour, until the meat is tender. Add the prunes, apricots and orange rind, put the lid on the tagine again, and simmer for a further 15–20 minutes. Stir in the honey, season with salt and pepper, cover, and simmer for a further 10 minutes. Make sure there is enough liquid in the pot as you want the sauce to be syrupy and slightly caramelized, but not dry. Stir in half of the fresh coriander, then serve immediately, sprinkled with the remaining coriander and accompanied by chunks of crusty bread or a mound of Plain, Buttery Couscous.

lamb tagine with shallots and dates
tajine bil tmar

3 tablespoons olive oil with a nut of butter, or ghee

700 g lean boned lamb, from the shoulder or neck, trimmed and cubed

12 shallots, peeled and left whole

4–6 garlic cloves, peeled and left whole

2 teaspoons ground turmeric

2 cinnamon sticks

1–2 tablespoons runny honey

225 g stoned, moist dates

1–2 tablespoons sesame seeds, toasted

sea salt and freshly ground black pepper

bread or Plain, Buttery Couscous (see page 77), to serve

Serves 4–6

Commonly known as the 'bread of the desert' the Arabs and the Berbers treat dates as a sacred food source as they and their ancestors have survived off them for generations, even when there has been little else to eat. They also symbolize hospitality and prosperity, so they are offered to guests and they are popped into numerous tagines and couscous dishes.

Heat the oil and the butter in the base of a tagine or in a heavy-based casserole. Toss the lamb in and brown it all over. Using a slotted spoon, remove the meat from the tagine and set aside. Add the shallots and garlic and sauté, stirring occasionally, until they begin to colour. Add the turmeric and cinnamon sticks and return the meat to the tagine. Pour in just enough water to cover the meat then bring it to the boil. Reduce the heat, cover with the lid and simmer for about 1 hour, giving it a stir from time to time.

Stir in the honey and season with salt and lots of black pepper. Add the dates, replace the lid, and cook for a further 25–30 minutes. Sprinkle with the toasted sesame seeds and serve with chunks of crusty bread or a mound of Plain, Buttery Couscous.

kefta tagine with lemon and coriander
tajine bil kefta

1 tablespoon olive oil

1 tablespoon butter, or ghee

1 onion, roughly chopped

2–3 garlic cloves, halved and smashed

a thumb-sized piece of fresh ginger, peeled and finely chopped

1 red chilli, deseeded and finely sliced

2 teaspoons ground turmeric

a small bunch of fresh coriander, chopped

freshly squeezed juice of 1 lemon

1 lemon, cut into 6 segments, pips removed

a small bunch of fresh mint leaves, chopped

bread, Plain, Buttery Couscous (see page 77) or a salad, to serve

For the *kefta*:

450 g finely minced lamb or beef

1 onion, finely chopped or grated

a small bunch of fresh flat leaf parsley, finely chopped

1–2 teaspoons ground cinnamon

1 teaspoon ground cumin

1 teaspoon ground coriander

½ teaspoon cayenne or 1 teaspoon paprika

sea salt and freshly ground black pepper

Serves 4–6

Light and lemony, this *kefta* tagine is quite different to many of the sweet and spicy tagines prepared with fruit. The *kefta* can be made ahead of time and kept in the refrigerator until ready to use. You can serve this tagine with chunks of fresh, crusty bread, couscous or a salad.

To make the kefta, pound the minced lamb or beef in a bowl with your hands by lifting it up and slapping it back down into the bowl to knock out the air. Add the onion, parsley and spices and season with salt and pepper. Again, using your hands, mix the ingredients together and knead well, pounding the mixture for a few minutes. Take pieces of the mixture and shape them into little walnut-sized balls. Set aside.

Heat the oil and butter in the base of a tagine or a heavy-based casserole. Stir in the onion, garlic, ginger and chilli and sauté until they begin to brown. Add the turmeric and half the coriander and pour in 300 ml water. Bring the water to the boil, reduce the heat and simmer, covered, for 10 minutes.

Carefully place the kefta in the liquid, put the lid back on and poach them for about 15 minutes, rolling them in the liquid from time to time. Pour over the lemon juice, season the liquid with salt and pepper and tuck the lemon segments around the kefta. Cover and poach gently for a further 10 minutes. Sprinkle with the mint and the rest of the coriander. Serve hot with bread, Plain, Buttery Couscous or a salad.

chicken tagine with preserved lemons, green olives and thyme
tajine djaj bi zaytoun wal hamid

1 organic chicken, about 1.5 kg

1 tablespoon olive oil with a nut of butter

2 preserved lemons, cut into strips (see page 11)

175 g cracked green olives

1–2 teaspoons dried thyme or oregano

a small bunch of fresh flat leaf parsley, finely chopped

bread or Lemon Couscous (see page 82), to serve

For the marinade:

1 onion, grated

3 garlic cloves, crushed

25 g fresh ginger, peeled and grated

a small bunch of fresh coriander, finely chopped

a pinch of saffron threads

freshly squeezed juice of 1 lemon

3–4 tablespoons olive oil

sea salt and freshly ground black pepper

Serves 4–6

This is another Moroccan classic employing two of the most traditional ingredients: cracked green olives and preserved lemon. Refreshing and tasty, this dish can be made with chicken joints or a whole chicken. Served with a lemon couscous and a side salad or vegetable dish, such as steamed carrots tossed with spices and mint, this is a delicious dish for lunch or supper.

In a bowl mix together all the ingredients for the marinade and rub it all over the inside and outside of the chicken. Cover and chill in the refrigerator for 1–2 hours.

Heat the olive oil and butter in the base of a tagine or a heavy-based casserole. Add the chicken and brown it on all sides. Tip in any left-over marinade and add enough water to come halfway up the sides of the chicken. Bring the water to the boil, reduce the heat and cover with a lid. Simmer for about 50 minutes, turning the chicken from time to time.

Add the preserved lemons, olives and half of the thyme. Cover with the lid again and simmer for a further 20 minutes. Check the seasoning and add some salt and pepper if necessary. Sprinkle the rest of the thyme and the parsley over the top. Serve from the tagine with fresh, crusty bread or Lemon Couscous and a salad or vegetable dish.

monkfish tagine with preserved lemon and mint
tajine bil samak

2–3 tablespoons olive oil

1 red onion, finely chopped

2 carrots, finely chopped

2 celery stalks, finely chopped

1 preserved lemon, finely chopped (see page 11)

1 x 400 g tin of plum tomatoes with the juice

300 ml fish stock or water

1 kg fresh monkfish tail, cut into large chunks

a bunch of fresh mint leaves, finely shredded

sea salt and freshly ground black pepper

bread or sautéed potatoes, to serve

For the *chermoula*:

2–3 garlic cloves, chopped

1 red chilli, deseeded and chopped

1 teaspoon sea salt

a small bunch of fresh coriander

a pinch of saffron fronds

1–2 teaspoons ground cumin

3–4 tablespoons olive oil

freshly squeezed juice of 1 lemon

Serves 4–6

The fresh fish tagines of the coastal areas are simply wonderful, redolent with spices and buttery sauces, often piquant with lemon and chillies and tempered with fresh herbs. Inland, fish tagines are prepared with freshwater fish, such as the local shad, and flavoured with the herbs of the region. The distinct Moroccan marinade, *chermoula*, is often employed in fish dishes as the flavours of chilli, cumin and coriander marry so well and complement the fish perfectly. Serve this tagine with chunks of fresh bread, or sautéed potatoes and a leafy salad.

First make the chermoula. Using a mortar and pestle pound the garlic and chilli with the salt to form a paste. Add the coriander leaves and pound to a coarse paste. Beat in the saffron fronds and cumin and bind well with the olive oil and lemon juice (you can whizz all the ingredients together in an electric blender, if you prefer). Reserve 2 teaspoons of the chermoula for cooking. Toss the monkfish in the remaining chermoula, cover and leave to marinate in the refrigerator for 1–2 hours.

Heat the oil in the base of a tagine or a heavy-based casserole. Stir in the onion, carrots and celery and sauté for 2–3 minutes, until softened. Stir in half the preserved lemon, the reserved 2 teaspoons of chermoula and the tomatoes. Cook gently for about 10 minutes to reduce the liquid, then add the stock. Bring the liquid to the boil, cover the tagine, reduce the heat and simmer for 10–15 minutes.

Add the monkfish to the tagine, cover with the lid and cook gently for 6–8 minutes, until the fish is cooked through. Season with salt and pepper, sprinkle with the remaining preserved lemon and the shredded mint and serve with chunks of fresh bread or sautéed potatoes and a leafy salad.

prawn tagine with saffron, ginger and fennel
tajine bil kimroun

4–5 tablespoons olive oil

20 raw king prawns, with heads removed

2 onions, finely chopped

2 garlic cloves, finely chopped

25 g fresh ginger, peeled and finely chopped

a pinch of saffron fronds

1–2 teaspoons smoked paprika

1 x 400 g tin of tomatoes, drained of juice

a small bunch of fresh coriander,
finely chopped

a small bunch of fresh flat leaf parsley,
finely chopped

1 teaspoon sugar

4 fennel bulbs, trimmed and sliced
thickly lengthways

sea salt and freshly ground black pepper

bread, to serve

Serves 4

Many shellfish tagines are not so much traditional as they are inspired by cultural influences, such as the prawn and mussel tagines of Tangier that resemble the cooking of Andalusia across the water. Serve this tagine as a first or second course with chunks of crusty bread.

Heat 2–3 tablespoons of the olive oil in the base of a tagine or a heavy-based casserole. Add the prawns and cook for 2–3 minutes, until they turn opaque. Using a slotted spoon, remove the prawns from the tagine and set aside. Keep the oil in the pan.

Stir the onion, garlic, ginger and saffron into the oil and sauté for 3–4 minutes, until they begin to colour. Add the paprika, tomatoes and half the herbs. Stir in the sugar and season with salt and pepper. Cook gently, partially covered, for about 10 minutes until the mixture thickens to form a sauce.

Meanwhile, steam the fennel for about 5 minutes, until it softens. Heat the remaining olive oil in a frying pan and add the steamed fennel. Cook gently on both sides for 4–5 minutes, until it turns golden. Sprinkle with salt and pepper.

Toss the cooked prawns in the tomato sauce, place the fennel on top, cover with the lid, and cook gently for 5 minutes. Sprinkle with the remaining coriander and parsley immediately before serving.

A Moroccan *k'dra* is a stew cooked in the traditional fermented butter, *smen* (which gives it its distinctive taste), in a large copper pot (a *k'dra*). The other feature of a *k'dra* is the large quantity of onions used in the dish. A *k'dra* is best served on its own, perhaps with a little bread, and wedges of lemon to squeeze over it, or with a mound of buttery couscous.

chicken *k'dra* with chickpeas, raisins and red peppers
k'dra djaj

1 organic chicken, about 1.5 kg, jointed into 6 pieces

175 g chickpeas, soaked in cold water for at least 6 hours and drained

6 onions, finely chopped

1–2 cinnamon sticks

2 pinches of saffron fronds

1 teaspoon sea salt

1 teaspoon freshly ground black pepper

2 red peppers

3–4 tablespoons olive oil

3–4 tablespoons golden raisins or sultanas

2 tablespoons smen, ghee or butter (see page 11)

a bunch of fresh flat leaf parsley, finely chopped

1 lemon, cut into wedges, to serve

bread or Plain, Buttery Couscous (see page 77), to serve

Serves 4–6

Put the chicken in a large heavy-based casserole. Add the chickpeas, 2 tablespoons of the chopped onion, the cinnamon sticks and saffron fronds and season with salt and pepper. Pour in enough water to cover the chicken and chickpeas by 2.5 cm and bring it to the boil. Cover the casserole, reduce the heat and cook gently for about 1 hour, checking the water level from time to time.

Meanwhile, preheat the oven to 180°C (350°F) Gas 4. Put the peppers in a baking dish and pour over the oil. Bake them in the preheated oven for about 30 minutes, until they are tender and the skin has buckled slightly. Remove them from the oven and leave them until they are cool enough to handle. Peel off the skin, cut the peppers in half lengthways, remove the stalk and seeds and cut the flesh into long strips. Set aside.

Check the chicken and chickpeas, both of which should be tender, and add the rest of the onions with the raisins, butter and half the parsley. Put the lid back on and cook gently for about 40 minutes, until the onions have almost formed a purée and there is very little liquid left.

Arrange the chicken joints on a serving dish and spoon the chickpeas, raisins and onions around them. Scatter the strips of pepper over the top and serve with lemon wedges to squeeze over and crusty bread or Plain, Buttery Couscous.

lamb *k'dra* with sweet potatoes and okra
k'dra bil batata

6–8 lamb shanks, trimmed and cut into bite-sized pieces

6 onions, halved lengthways and sliced crossways

a pinch of saffron fronds

2 cinnamon sticks

1 teaspoon ground black pepper

2 medium sweet potatoes, peeled, halved lengthways and thickly sliced

2 tablespoons smen, ghee or butter (see page 11)

250 g fresh okra

freshly squeezed juice of 1 lemon

sea salt

bread or Plain, Buttery Couscous (see page 77), to serve

Serves 6–8

This is a Berber dish which is often prepared with large cuts of meat, such as shanks, knuckle or sheeps' heads, which are removed at the end of the cooking and arranged around a mound of couscous. The vegetables are arranged on top and the cooking broth is served separately to spoon over the dish. Traditionally the meat is cooked in a large pot below the couscous.

Put the lamb pieces in a large heavy-based casserole with half of the onions, saffron, cinnamon sticks and black pepper. Pour in enough water to cover the meat and bring it to the boil. Reduce the heat, cover with a lid and simmer gently for about 1½ hours (top up with water if necessary).

Add the sweet potatoes, the smen and the rest of the onions. Simmer for a further 20–25 minutes, until the potatoes are tender. Meanwhile, toss the okra in the lemon juice, leave for 10 minutes, then drain. Add the okra to the casserole and simmer for a further 5–10 minutes, until the okra is cooked through but still retains a crunch. Season to taste with salt and serve with crusty bread or Plain, Buttery Couscous.

the art of making couscous

Mint tea may be Morocco's national drink, but couscous is the country's national dish. It is prepared throughout Morocco and is a traditional staple of the whole of the North African region, right down to Senegal and across to Chad. Further east in Egypt and parts of the Middle East, it is known as *moghrabiyyeh*, 'the dish of the North Africans'. Although referred to as a 'grain', couscous is not technically one; instead it could be more accurately described as Moroccan 'pasta' as it is made with semolina flour and water and then hand-rolled and dried even though it is prepared and served like rice.

Couscous is of fundamental value to Moroccan culture for dietary, religious and symbolic reasons, as Moroccans believe it is a food that brings God's blessing upon those who consume it. It is therefore prepared in every household on Muslim holy days and on Fridays, the Islamic day of rest, when it is traditionally distributed to the poor as well. For the feast of Achoura, which commemorates the death of the Prophet's grandson, superstitious wives hide juicy morsels of sheeps' tail, which has been fried in its own fat and preserved, inside a mound of steaming couscous. This delicacy, called *qaddid,* is reputed to ensure the fidelity of the husbands. At festive and religious feasts, such as the traditional *diffas* to celebrate births and weddings, or the Berber *moussems*, a mound of couscous is served as the magnificent crown to end the meal. There is a Moroccan saying that 'each granule of couscous represents a good deed', so it is not surprising that thousands of granules are consumed in a day.

There are many different types of couscous in Morocco, some made with wheat flour, others with barley, maize or millet. In the rural areas, the village women still buy sacks of wheat, which they take to the local mill to be ground to semolina, and then laboriously prepare couscous every week by sprinkling the semolina flour with water and raking it with their fingers in a circular motion to form tiny balls. The balls are then rubbed against the side of the bowl using the palm of the hand and passed through a sieve to form a uniform size: *kesksou* (also *seksu* and *kuskusu*) is 2 mm in diameter; *seffa* or *mefuf* is ultra-fine at 1 mm in diameter and is mainly reserved for fillings and sweet dishes; and *mhammsa* is 3 mm in diameter. The tiny granules are then spread out to dry before use. In modern households in the cities, many cooks prefer to avoid this labour-intensive process and buy sacks of ready-prepared couscous which needs to be steamed several times before eating. Outside Morocco and the rest of the Maghreb, the most commonly available packets of couscous have been taken one step further as they are already precooked and only require soaking in water to swell, before being fluffed up and aerated using fingers and olive oil. (The recipes in this book use this precooked version, which is available in supermarkets and specialist shops). A standard measurement for these easy-to-use granules is roughly 500 g couscous to 500–600 ml warm salted water.

The preparation of couscous varies from region to region and is dependent on the type of granules, but the principal method involves placing the dried granules in a *ga'saa* – a wide, flat earthenware dish – and sprinkling them liberally with water. The moistened granules are then transferred to the metal *keskess*, a colander, and set snugly atop a *q'draa*, a large tin-lined, copper pot, which contains water or a stew of meat or vegetables. The utensils together are known in French as the two-tiered pot, the *couscoussière* – the term employed by the *pied-noir* communities, and the name that is used in international culinary circles. The steam between the *keskess* and the *q'draa* is sealed with a piece of cloth which is dipped in a mixture of flour and water. The couscous is then steamed, uncovered, until puffs of vapour emanate from the granules. The warm couscous is then returned to the *ga'saa* and mixed with more water before being returned to the colander and steamed a second time until the granules become soft and plump. Finally it is flavoured with lashings of butter, olive oil or smen, which is rubbed into the grains with the fingertips, and it is moistened with the broth from the stew. This preparation plays such an important role in the culinary life of most Moroccans that it determines the status of a cook's ability. The word 'couscous' refers to the granules as well as the finished dish, which should be light and airy, almost floating above the plate and heavenly to touch and taste. If you manage to make a Moroccan swoon over your couscous, you will have received the greatest compliment of all.

To the majority of Moroccans a meal would be unthinkable without couscous. It is extremely versatile and is traditionally served as a course on its own, but it can also be served as an accompaniment to tagines or grilled and roasted meats. It can look spectacular, particularly when piled up in a cone-shaped mound for banquets and topped with stuffed pigeons, dates and almonds, or decorated with strips of colourful vegetables and topped with sweet onions and raisins tinged yellow with saffron and it is often accompanied by little side dishes, such as spicy chickpeas, marinated raisins and harissa paste. Eating couscous in a traditional manner is an experience in itself and requires a little practice. It is a communal dish so, once the mound has been set on the ground, or on a low table, diners literally ram their right hands, palm upwards, into the grains to extract a handful and then, using the thumb and first two fingers, deftly roll the grains to form small tight balls that might incorporate some small pieces of meat or vegetables, and flip them into their mouths. It looks easy but, on first attempts, the sauce dribbles down your wrist and the granules spill all over the table!

Traditionally, plain, buttery couscous, piled high in a mound, is served as a dish on its own after a tagine or roasted meat. It is held in such high esteem that religious feasts and celebratory meals would be unthinkable with it. The par-boiled couscous available outside Morocco is extremely easy to prepare, making it a practical accompaniment for many dishes.

plain, buttery couscous
kesksou

350 g couscous, rinsed and drained

½ teaspoon sea salt

400 ml warm water

2 tablespoons sunflower or olive oil

25 g butter, broken into little pieces

For the top:

15 g butter

2–3 tablespoons blanched, flaked almonds

Serves 4–6

Preheat the oven to 180°C (350°F) Gas 4. Tip the couscous into an ovenproof dish. Stir the salt into the water and pour it over the couscous. Leave the couscous to absorb the water for about 10 minutes.

Using your fingers, rub the oil into the couscous grains to break up the lumps and aerate them. Scatter the butter over the surface and cover with a piece of foil or wet greaseproof paper. Put the dish in the preheated oven for about 15 minutes, until the couscous is heated through. Meanwhile, prepare the almonds. Melt the butter in a heavy-based frying pan over medium heat, add the almonds and cook, stirring until they begin to turn golden. Remove from the pan and drain on kitchen paper.

Take the couscous out of the oven and fluff up the grains with a fork. Serve it from the dish or tip it onto a plate and pile it high in a mound, with the almonds scattered over the top.

This is a traditional couscous dish, which would be made in a *couscoussière* with the meat cooking in the bottom compartment creating the steam for the couscous above. However, the parboiled couscous can be prepared separately and the whole dish combined at the end. The *tfaia* is a sweet cinnamon and saffron mixture of onions and raisins that is spooned on top of the stew.

couscous *tfaia* with beef
kesksou tfaia

750 g beef rump or chuck, cut into cubes

1 onion, chopped

1 teaspoon ground coriander

1 teaspoon ground cumin

a pinch of saffron fronds

500 g couscous

½ teaspoon sea salt

500 ml warm water

1–2 tablespoons olive oil

15 g butter

For the *tfaia*:

1–2 tablespoons olive oil

25 g butter

4 onions, thinly sliced

1–2 teaspoons cinnamon

1 teaspoon ground ginger

1 teaspoon saffron fronds, soaked in
2 tablespoons warm water

2 tablespoons honey

3 tablespoons golden raisins, soaked in warm water for 15 minutes and drained

sea salt and freshly ground black pepper

Serves 4–6

Preheat the oven to 180ºC (350ºF) Gas 4. Put the beef in the base of a tagine or heavy-based casserole with the onion, spices and saffron. Pour in just enough water to cover the meat, then bring it to the boil. Reduce the heat, cover with a lid and leave to simmer for about 1 hour.

Meanwhile, prepare the couscous. Tip it into an ovenproof dish. Stir the salt into the water and pour it over the couscous. Leave the couscous to absorb the water for about 10 minutes. Using your fingers, rub the oil into the couscous grains to break up the lumps and aerate them. Scatter the butter over the surface and cover with a piece of foil or wet greaseproof paper. Put the dish in the preheated oven for about 15 minutes, until the couscous is heated through.

Prepare the tfaia. Heat the oil and butter in a heavy-based saucepan. Add the onions and sauté them for 1–2 minutes, until softened. Reduce the heat and add the spices, saffron water, honey and season to taste with salt and pepper. Cover with a lid and cook gently for 15–20 minutes. Stir in the raisins and cook, uncovered, for a further 10 minutes.

Tip the couscous onto a serving dish in a mound and create a well in the top. Using a slotted spoon, transfer the meat into the well and top with the tfaia. Strain the cooking liquid from the meat and serve it separately as a sauce to spoon or pour over the couscous.

This is a lovely spring or summer dish as it is prepared with the young green vegetables in season, such as fresh broad beans and peas, artichokes, asparagus, rocket leaves, spring onions and baby courgettes. You can serve this as a course on its own, or as an accompaniment to many tagines and grilled meat dishes.

green couscous with a spring broth
kesksou l'hodra

500 g couscous
½ teaspoon sea salt
600 ml warm water
1–2 tablespoons olive oil
15 g butter
1 litre vegetable or chicken stock
350 g fresh broad beans, shelled
200 g fresh peas, shelled
12 spring onions, trimmed and thickly sliced
6 baby courgettes, thickly sliced
4–6 globe artichoke hearts, cut into quarters
a bunch of fresh flat leaf parsley, finely chopped
a bunch of fresh coriander leaves, finely chopped
a bunch of fresh mint leaves, finely chopped
sea salt and freshly ground black pepper

Serves 4–6

Preheat the oven to 200°C (400°F) Gas 6. Tip the couscous into an ovenproof dish. Stir the salt into the water and pour it over the couscous. Leave the couscous to absorb the water for about 10 minutes. Using your fingers, rub the oil into the couscous grains to break up the lumps and aerate them. Scatter the butter over the surface and cover with a piece of foil or wet greaseproof paper. Put the dish in the preheated oven for about 15 minutes, until the couscous is heated through.

Meanwhile, prepare the vegetable broth. Pour the stock into a heavy-based saucepan and bring it to the boil. Add the broad beans, peas, spring onions, courgettes and artichokes and cook for 5–10 minutes, until tender. Season the broth with salt and pepper and stir in the herbs.

Remove the couscous from the oven and tip it onto a serving plate. Using a slotted spoon, lift the vegetables out of the broth and arrange them around, or over, the mound of couscous. Moisten with a little broth, then pour the rest into a bowl or jug and serve it separately to spoon or pour over the couscous.

lemon couscous with roasted vegetables
kesksou bil laymoun

8 baby aubergines, left whole

3–4 small courgettes, cut into 4 lengthways

2 red peppers, with stalk and seeds removed, and cut into 4 lengthways

4 garlic cloves, peeled and cut into 4 lengthways

a thumb-sized piece of fresh ginger, cut into thin sticks

100 ml olive oil

sea salt

a bunch of fresh coriander, coarsely chopped

a bunch of fresh mint, coarsely chopped

For the Lemon Couscous:

500 g couscous

½ teaspoon sea salt

600 ml warm water

1–2 tablespoons olive oil

1 preserved lemon, finely chopped (see page 11)

15 g butter

Serves 4

This is a modern recipe and ideal for vegetarians. For a variation, instead of roasting the vegetables, you could prepare vegetable kebabs on the barbecue and serve them with the couscous. Generally, aubergines, courgettes and peppers are roasted together but you can vary the vegetables, according to the season.

Preheat the oven to 200°C (400°F) Gas 6. Put the vegetables, garlic and ginger in an ovenproof dish. Pour over the oil, sprinkle with salt and cook in the preheated oven for about 40 minutes, until they vegetables are tender and nicely browned.

To make the lemon couscous, tip the couscous into an ovenproof dish. Stir the salt into the water and pour it over the couscous. Leave it to absorb the water for about 10 minutes. Using your fingers, rub the oil into the couscous grains to break up the lumps and aerate them. Toss in the preserved lemon, scatter the butter over the surface and cover with a piece of foil or wet greaseproof paper. Put the dish in the oven for about 15 minutes, until the couscous has heated through.

Tip the couscous onto a serving plate in a mound. Arrange the vegetables over and around it and spoon some of the roasting oil over the top. Sprinkle with the coriander and mint and serve immediately.

grills, pan-fries and roasts

kefta kebabs with *harissa* couscous
kefta kabob

For the kebabs:

500 g finely minced lean lamb or beef

1 onion, finely chopped

2 garlic cloves, crushed

1–2 teaspoons ground cinnamon

1–2 teaspoons Ras-el-Hanout (see page 93)

1 teaspoon sea salt

a small bunch of fresh flat leaf parsley, finely chopped

a small bunch of fresh coriander, finely chopped

For the Harissa Couscous:

225 g couscous

225 ml warm water

½ teaspoon sea salt

1 tablespoon olive oil

2–3 teaspoons Harissa (see page 11)

25 g butter, broken into small pieces

a barbecue or charcoal grill
8–12 metal or wooden skewers

Serves 4–6

Another popular street dish throughout Morocco, these minced meat kebabs vary from vendor to vendor, each with his own liberal pinch of spice or bunch of herbs. As the national spice *ras-el-hanout* is open to personal creation, the exact flavouring of some of these *kefta* kebabs can be quite difficult to detect.

To make the kebabs, mix the minced meat with the other ingredients and knead well, lifting the mixture up and slapping it back into the bowl to knock out the air, until it is smooth but slightly sticky. Cover and chill in the refrigerator for about 1–2 hours to allow the flavours to mingle.

Meanwhile, prepare the couscous. Tip the couscous into a large bowl. Stir the salt into the water and pour it over the couscous, stirring all the time so that the water is absorbed evenly. Leave the couscous to swell for about 10 minutes then, using your fingers, rub the oil and the harissa into the couscous.

Preheat the oven to 180°C (350°F) Gas 4 for the couscous and prepare the barbecue for the kebabs. Divide the kebab mixture into 8–12 portions and mould them into fat sausage shapes. Insert a skewer through each one.

Tip the couscous into an ovenproof dish and scatter the butter over the surface and cover with a piece of foil or wet greaseproof paper. Put the dish in the preheated oven for 15 minutes, until the couscous is heated through. Place the kebabs on the barbecue and cook for 4–5 minutes on each side. Serve immediately.

souk kebabs with roasted cumin and paprika
shish kabob

This is street food at its best. Quick, tasty and spicy, kebabs like these are cooked by street vendors all over Morocco. The enticing aroma of charcoal-grilled meat and roasted cumin in the souks and medinas of Fes and Marrakesh wafts around every corner and through the labyrinthine streets. Also known by their French name, *brochettes*, these kebabs are often served tucked into flat bread pouches with a dollop of tomato salsa or *harissa*.

1–2 onions, grated

2 teaspoons sea salt

450 g lean shoulder of lamb, trimmed and cut into bite-sized cubes

freshly squeezed juice of 1 lemon

2 teaspoons cumin seeds, roasted and ground

1–2 teaspoons paprika

a small bunch of fresh flat leaf parsley, finely chopped

a small bunch of fresh coriander leaves, finely chopped

freshly ground black pepper

1 lemon, cut into wedges, to serve

a barbecue or charcoal grill

4 metal or wooden skewers

Serves 4

Put the grated onion in a bowl and sprinkle with the sea salt. Leave it to 'weep' for 10 minutes, then force it through a nylon sieve, or squeeze it with your hand, to extract the juice.

Put the lamb in a bowl and pour over the extracted onion juice. Add the lemon juice, roasted cumin, paprika, herbs and black pepper, to taste. Toss well so that the meat is thoroughly coated in the marinade. Cover and chill in the refrigerator for at least 2 hours, or overnight, to allow the flavours to penetrate the meat.

Prepare the barbecue. Thread the marinated meat onto skewers and place them on the barbecue. Cook for 3–4 minutes on each side until cooked through and serve immediately with wedges of lemon to squeeze over them.

the souks, spices and sensual flavours

'Come and see the donkey parking', urged a friendly Berber dressed in a chocolate-brown *djellaba*, as he led us through the crowds of rural men, haggling over sheep and vegetables. He had thought my children were getting bored of hanging around the food stalls, while I asked endless questions, so the 'donkey parking' would cheer them up. Meandering through the narrow lanes, we arrived at the back of the market where men were grilling cuts of meat over charcoal stoves, the rest of the carcass lying on the ground at their feet – head, guts, hooves – and on we went through a tunnel-like tea house to a small square window at the back through which we shoved our heads to admire the sheer drop to the river below, beside which hundreds of donkeys were patiently standing waiting for their owners. In the morning, they had brought goods to the market and later that day they would return home with more strapped to their backs – a familiar sight on the Moroccan culinary landscape.

The country markets and the souks of the old Medinas are the lungs of Morocco. Magical and enticing, filled with arresting aromas – some pleasant, others not – they are bustling venues for haggling, meal planning, utensil buying, snacking, conducting business, entertainment and gossip. The crowds, the chaos, the noise, the smells, the donkeys and camels, the tooting trucks and mopeds, and the labyrinthine passageways all add to the excitement of shopping. From the medieval souks of Fes and Marrakesh to the Berber markets in the foothills of the Atlas Mountains, there is a sense of living life close to the ground. A local stone is used for shampoo; a murky-looking sludge is sold as soap; tiny clay saucers are offered as lipstick – if you wet your finger you can apply the natural colour to your lips; ground plants, insects and lizards are sought after as aphrodisiacs. You can buy the freshly stripped fleece of a lamb; the decapitated head of a cow; the skin of a python; tiny live tortoises; and dried chameleons.

To experience the chaos, diversity and food all in one place, it is worth visiting the Place Djemma el Fna, known as the 'Assembly of the Dead', after the heads of conspirators were displayed there by one of the sultans. Situated at the heart of Marrakesh, it is a wide open area combining theatre and street food, surrounded by the ancient souks selling jewellery and leather slippers, colourful kaftans and belly dance outfits, drums and water pipes and, if you venture deeper, you will come across hidden pockets of olives and olive oil; brightly coloured jars of preserved lemons and pickled vegetables; bunches of luscious green herbs; crates of dried apricots, prunes, dates and figs; pistachios, walnuts and almonds; buckets of runny honey, and carts of seasonal fruit and vegetables, such as aubergines, courgettes, oranges and watermelons. By mid-afternoon the Place takes on the atmosphere of a carnival with the beating of drums and bells, the snake charmers and performing monkeys, and the fire-eaters and storytellers, while the smoke of the makeshift stoves wafts behind them with the intense smell of kebabs, *kefta*, fried fish, hot breads and pastries. The aroma is one of smoke combined with burning frankincense, bursts of citrus fruit interspersed with fresh coriander and mint, and heady with spices, such as cumin, cinnamon, turmeric, paprika and ginger.

Moroccan cooks use every spice that ever found its way across the Sahara desert or over the Mediterranean, blending the influences of the different cultures that have left their culinary mark: Berber, Arab, Moorish, Jewish, French, Ottoman and Spanish. The cooking in the imperial kitchens of the Berber dynasties relied on a delicate marriage of olive oil and spices and some of the best examples of this are to be found in Fassia cooking, the dishes from Fes, whereas rural Berber cooking tends to be more pungent and fiery with powerful tones of cumin, ginger, and turmeric, flavoured with *smen*. Honey and sugar, and in some cases icing sugar, are added to dishes to enhance the flavour or to add a sweet note; black pepper is used as a spice, not just as a seasoning, to mitigate the sweetness of a dish; cumin is believed to stimulate the appetite and ginger is reputed to aid digestion, so both these spices are added in generous quantities. Paprika and chilli add a burst of fire in certain dishes and cinnamon acts as a delightfully warming component in sweet tagines and sweet and savoury pastries. Spice mixtures for *kefta* often include coriander and cumin seeds ground with paprika and allspice, whereas soup spice mixtures consist of ginger, cumin and caraway. Saffron plays an integral part in Moroccan cooking but, although it is cultivated in the south, it is expensive, so a cheap grade of ground saffron mixed with wild flowers, or ground turmeric, are used as 'poor man's saffron' for colouring. The scented waters of orange blossom and rose petals are splashed frequently into salads and sweet dishes and they are used to refresh the hands before and after eating. Of all the Moroccan spices and flavourings, the one that stands above all the rest is *ras-el-hanout*, literally 'the head of the shop'. A legendary mix of at least thirty different spices, it is the soul of Moroccan cooking. The story behind it claims that a warrior, presumably one of the Arab invaders, created the mix with all the scents and flavours of the countries he had passed through. Rich in flavour and known to contain various aphrodisiacs, as well as several unknown ingredients, each spice merchant has his own recipe and the price will vary according to the rarity of the spices included. Beyond the souks and the barks, seeds and leaves from deepest Africa, it is impossible to recreate the complexity and eloquence of genuine *ras-el-hanout*, but the recipe on the following page conjures up a taste of the real thing.

ras-el-hanout

1 teaspoon black peppercorns
1 teaspoon cloves
1 teaspoon aniseeds
1 teaspoon nigella seeds
1 teaspoon allspice berries
1 teaspoon cardamom seeds
2 teaspoons ground ginger
2 teaspoons ground turmeric
2 teaspoons coriander seeds
2 pieces mace
2 pieces cinnamon bark
2 teaspoons dried mint
1 dried red chilli
1 teaspoon dried lavender
6 dried rosebuds, broken up

Makes approximately 4–5 tablespoons

Using a mortar and pestle, or an electric blender, grind together all the spices to form a coarse powder. Stir in the lavender and rose petals and tip the mixture into an airtight container. You can store this spice mix for up to 6 months if you keep it away from direct sunlight.

Traditionally, this is a festive dish, as an entire lamb or kid is roasted slowly over embers over a pit dug in the ground and shared among a community or a large family. It is generally prepared in this way for holy days, such as Aid el Adha, to celebrate the near-sacrifice of Isaac, and it is one of the dishes cooked for the Jewish *hilloula* and the Muslim *moussem*, which are both festive celebrations to mark a religious or significant event, such as a marriage or the death of a saint. When cooking a joint of lamb in a communal oven, Moroccan cooks often add seasonal fruit, such as fresh figs, plums, apricots or quince to the dish – this is a delightful option for you too.

roasted *smen*-coated lamb with honey
mechoui

a leg of lamb, about 2 kg

200 ml water

2–3 tablespoons runny honey

10–12 pieces of fresh fruit, such as figs, plums or apricots (optional)

a bunch of fresh coriander leaves, roughly chopped

sea salt and freshly ground black pepper

For the *smen* coating:

4 garlic cloves, chopped

40 g fresh ginger, peeled and chopped

1 red chilli, deseeded and chopped

a generous pinch of sea salt

a small bunch each of fresh coriander and flat leaf parsley, chopped

1–2 teaspoons ground cumin

1–2 teaspoons ground coriander

3 tablespoons smen, softened butter or olive oil (see page 11)

To serve:

Plain, Buttery Couscous (see page 77)

a handful of chopped almonds and pistachios (optional)

a large roasting dish or tray

Serves 6

First, make the smen coating. Using a mortar and pestle, pound the garlic, ginger and chilli with enough salt to form a coarse paste. Add the fresh coriander and parsley, pound to a paste and stir in the ground cumin and coriander. Put the smen in a bowl and beat in the paste until thoroughly mixed. Cut small incisions in the leg of lamb with a sharp knife and rub the spicy smen all over the meat, making sure it goes into the incisions. Cover and leave in the refrigerator for at least 2 hours.

Preheat the oven to 200°C (400°F) Gas 4. Transfer the leg of lamb to a roasting dish and pour the water around it. Roast in the preheated oven for about 1 hour 15 minutes, basting from time to time, until it is nicely browned. Spoon the honey over the lamb and place the fresh figs, plums or apricots around the meat, if using. Return the dish to the oven a further 15 minutes.

Put the roasted lamb in a serving dish and leave it to rest for about 15 minutes before serving. Meanwhile, heat the juices in the roasting dish, season with salt and pepper, and pour over the roast lamb. Sprinkle the coriander over the top and, if using fruit, arrange it around the dish. Serve accompanied by a mound of Plain, Buttery Couscous tossed with chopped almonds and pistachios.

Throughout Morocco whole chickens are generally spit-roasted, grilled over charcoal or cooked in large tagines. Oven-roasting tends to be the method employed in the contemporary kitchens of the big towns and cities. Stuffed with aromatic, fruity couscous, this dish is really a meal on its own, accompanied by a salad.

roast chicken stuffed with couscous, apricots and dates
djaj m'ammar bil kesksou

2 garlic cloves, crushed

2 teaspoons dried oregano or thyme

1–2 teaspoons paprika

2 tablespoons butter, softened

1 large organic chicken, about 1.5 kg

1 sliced off orange end ·

150 ml chicken stock

For the couscous stuffing:

225 g couscous

½ teaspoon salt

225 ml warm water

1 tablespoon olive oil

1–2 teaspoons ground cinnamon

1 teaspoon ground coriander

½ teaspoon ground cumin

1 tablespoon runny honey

2 tablespoons golden raisins

125 g ready-to-eat dried apricots, thickly sliced

125 g ready-to-eat dates, thickly sliced or chopped

2–3 tablespoons blanched almonds, roasted

Serves 4–6

Preheat the oven to 180°C (350°F) Gas 4. To make the stuffing, tip the couscous into a large bowl. Stir the salt into the warm water and pour it over the couscous, stirring all the time so that the water is absorbed evenly. Leave the couscous to swell for about 10 minutes then, using your fingers, rub the oil into the couscous to break up the lumps and aerate it. Stir in the other stuffing ingredients and set aside.

In a small bowl, beat the garlic, oregano and paprika into the softened butter then smear it all over the chicken, inside and out. Put the chicken in the base of a tagine or in an ovenproof dish and fill the cavity with as much of the couscous stuffing as you can (any left-over couscous can be heated through in the oven before serving and fluffed up with a little extra oil or butter). Seal the cavity with the slice of orange (you can squeeze the juice from the rest of the orange over the chicken). Pour the stock into the base of the tagine and roast the chicken in the oven for 1–1½ hours, basting from time to time, until the chicken is cooked.

Remove the chicken from the oven and allow it to rest for 10 minutes before carving or jointing it and strain the cooking juices into a jug. Heat up any remaining couscous (as described above) and serve this with the chicken, the jug of cooking juices to pour over and a green salad.

grilled sardine sandwiches stuffed with *chermoula*

sardines mzouwej

8 large or 16 small fresh sardines, gutted and boned with heads removed (you can ask the fishmonger to do this for you)

1 egg, beaten

sea salt

1 lemon, cut into quarters, to serve

For the chermoula:

2–3 garlic cloves, chopped

1 red chilli, deseeded and chopped

1 teaspoon sea salt

a small bunch each of fresh coriander and flat leaf parsley, chopped

2 teaspoons ground cumin

2 teaspoons paprika

4–5 tablespoons olive oil

freshly squeezed juice of 1 lemon

a barbecue or charcoal grill

Serves 4

The classic Moroccan marinade for fish called *chermoula* varies from cook to cook but gives the dishes a very distinct taste. In this dish the sardines are boned and butterflied and sandwiched together with the *chermoula* filling. Extremely fresh and tasty, the sardines can be grilled or fried and are best enjoyed on their own with a little lemon to squeeze over them.

Prepare the barbecue. To make the chermoula, use a mortar and pestle to pound the garlic and chilli with the salt to form a paste. Add the coriander and parsley leaves and pound to a coarse paste. Beat in the cumin and paprika and bind well with the olive oil and lemon juice (you can whizz all the ingredients together in an electric blender, if you prefer).

Open out the sardines and place half of them skin-side down on a flat surface. Smear the chermoula over the sardines and brush the sides with beaten egg. Place the remaining butterflied sardines on top to sandwich the mixture together. Place them on the heated barbecue and cook for 2–3 minutes on each side. Sprinkle with salt and serve immediately with the lemon wedges to squeeze over them.

pan-fried snapper with *harissa* and olive sauce
hout bil harissa

Fresh fish is often grilled or fried at stalls in the street and served with bread, or a little fiery sauce. You can use any firm-fleshed fish, such as snapper, sea bream, sea bass, monkfish or trout for this dish, which is delicious served on its own with chunks of bread to mop up the sauce.

To make the sauce, heat the oil in a heavy-based saucepan. Stir in the onion and garlic and cook for 2–3 minutes, until they begin to take on a little colour. Stir in the harissa, cinnamon stick and sugar and add the tomatoes. Cook for 4–5 minutes then add the olives and season to taste with salt and pepper. Remove from the heat and cover the pan to keep the sauce hot.

Season the flour with salt and pepper and toss the fish chunks in it. Heat the oil in a frying pan, add the fish chunks and fry them for about 2 minutes on each side, until golden brown. Drain the fish chunks on kitchen paper and transfer them to a serving dish. Spoon the sauce over and around the fish and sprinkle with parsley. Serve with wedges of lemon to squeeze over the fish.

2–3 tablespoons plain flour

2–3 fresh snapper, skinned and cut into chunks

sunflower oil, for shallow frying

a small bunch of fresh flat leaf parsley, coarsely chopped

sea salt and freshly ground black pepper

1 lemon, cut into wedges, to serve

bread, to serve

For the sauce:

2–3 tablespoons olive oil

1 onion, chopped

2 garlic cloves, chopped

1–2 teaspoons Harissa (see page 11)

1 cinnamon stick

2 teaspoons sugar

1 x 400 ml tin of chopped tomatoes, drained of juice

2–3 tablespoons black or kalamata olives

Serves 4

pan-fried prawns with ginger, cumin and paprika
langoustines piquantes

3 tablespoons olive oil

2–3 garlic cloves, chopped

25 g fresh ginger, peeled and grated

1 chilli, deseeded and chopped

1 teaspoon cumin seeds

1 teaspoon paprika

500 g raw king or Dublin bay prawns, shelled but with their tails intact

a bunch of fresh coriander, finely chopped

sea salt and freshly ground black pepper

1 lemon, cut into wedges, to serve

bread, to serve

Serves 4

This is a quick, easy way of preparing prawns for a snack or a main meal. Simply serve the juicy, piquant prawns from the cooking vessel with chunks of crusty bread to mop up the oil and spices left behind.

Heat the oil in the base of a tagine or a wide, heavy-based frying pan. Stir in the garlic, ginger, chilli and cumin seeds. As soon as a lovely aroma rises from the pan, add the paprika and toss in the prawns. Fry quickly over medium heat, until the prawns are just cooked and have turned opaque. Season to taste with salt and pepper and sprinkle with coriander. Serve the prawns immediately with the lemon wedges to squeeze over them.

Cooking fish with dates is a lovely Moroccan tradition. Trout and shad are often selected for this dish, which can be cooked in a tagine on the stove or in the oven. Cooking fish in this manner is often reserved for banquets and family celebrations where the whole fish is displayed with dates stuffed with almond paste.

baked trout stuffed with dates
samak mechoui

4 small or 2 large fresh trout, gutted, rinsed and patted dry

3 tablespoons olive oil with a nut of butter, or 2 tablespoons ghee

1 onion, finely chopped

25 g fresh ginger, peeled and finely chopped

2–3 teaspoons ground cinnamon plus 1 teaspoon for dusting

2–3 tablespoons blanched almonds, finely chopped

100 g medium- or short-grain rice, rinsed and drained

200 g moist, ready-to-eat dates, chopped

a small bunch of fresh coriander leaves, finely chopped

a small bunch of fresh flat leaf parsley, finely chopped

1 orange, cut into thin slices

sea salt and freshly ground black pepper

a large, shallow baking dish

Serve 4

Preheat the oven to 180ºC (350ºF) Gas 4. Using a sharp knife, slit the trout open along the belly and season the cavities with salt and pepper. Line an ovenproof dish with plenty of foil, so that the fish can be wrapped in it, and place the fish side by side on the foil.

Heat most of the oil and butter or ghee in a heavy-based saucepan. Stir in the onion and ginger and cook for 2–3 minutes, until they begin to colour. Stir in the cinnamon and almonds, add the rice and season to taste with salt and pepper. Pour in just enough water to cover the rice and bring it to the boil. Reduce the heat and simmer gently until all the water has been absorbed. Turn off the heat, cover the pan and leave the rice to steam for 10 minutes.

Add the dates, coriander and parsley to the rice and let it cool before stuffing the fish with it. To do this, spoon the filling into the cavities and brush the tops of the fish with the remaining oil or ghee. Place the orange slices around the fish, wrap up the foil to form a package, and place the dish in the preheated oven for 15–20 minutes. Open the foil and bake for a further 5 minutes, to lightly brown the top. Decorate the fish with a thin line of ground cinnamon by rubbing it between your thumb and index finger. Serve immediately.

char-grilled quails with kumquats

saman mechosi

This is great finger food, ideal for a barbecue. Generally pigeons, quails and poussins are cooked this way and served straight from the grill with bread. As the quails in this recipe are boned, you can easily slip them into the pocket of a pita bread, or you can serve them with any crunchy Moroccan salad.

4 quails, cleaned and boned (you can ask your butcher to do this)

2–3 tablespoons olive oil

freshly squeezed juice of 1 orange

25 g fresh ginger, peeled and grated

a pinch of saffron fronds

225 g kumquats, halved

2 tablespoons runny honey

1 teaspoon paprika

a bunch of fresh coriander leaves, roughly chopped

12 wooden skewers, soaked in water for 20 minutes or 12 metal skewers
a barbecue or charcoal grill

Serves 4

Thread 1 skewer through the wings of each quail and a second skewer through the thighs, so that each quail has 2 skewers through it. Put the quails in a shallow dish.

Mix the olive oil, orange juice, ginger and saffron together in a bowl and smear the mixture over the quails. Cover with cling film and place in the refrigerator for 2–3 hours, turning the quails in the marinade from time to time.

Meanwhile, prepare the barbecue and thread the kumquats onto the remaining skewers. Place the quails on the barbecue, brushing them with any leftover marinade, and cook them for about 4 minutes on each side. Halfway through the cooking time, put the kumquats on the barbecue with the quails and cook them until they become slightly charred.

Remove the quails and kumquats from the barbecue and serve immediately, drizzled with honey and sprinkled with the paprika and chopped coriander.

grilled *harissa* chicken

djaj bil harissa

Along with the ubiquitous lamb kebabs, street vendors sell chicken kebabs and *harissa*-coated chicken drumsticks and wings. Eaten on the hop with a lick of the fingers, grilled chicken is very popular in rural communities. Served as part of a barbecue at home, the drumsticks can be wrapped in paper or coriander to hold, or served with a salad such as the refreshing Carrot and Cumin Salad with Orange Flower Water (see page 18).

1–2 tablespoons Harissa (see page 11)

4 tablespoons olive oil

8–12 chicken drumsticks

a bunch of fresh coriander leaves on their stalks (optional)

sea salt

a barbecue or charcoal grill

Serves 4

Put the harissa in a bowl and stir in the olive oil until blended. Season with salt, if necessary, and smear the mixture over the chicken. Cover and chill in the refrigerator for about 2 hours.

Prepare the barbecue. Place the marinated drumsticks on the barbecue and cook for about 4–5 minutes on each side. Wrap them in coriander to serve, if using, and tuck in immediately.

This is a delicious way to cook duck, or you could try it with lamb. Overall, the dish is succulent and very sweet, so you could alter the amount of honey and sugar to your taste. Serve the duck with plain couscous and a tart salad to cut through the sweetness.

roast duck with honey, pears and figs
bata bil bouawid

25 g fresh ginger, peeled and chopped

2 garlic cloves, chopped

2–3 tablespoons olive oil

4 duck legs, skin on

2 pears, cored and cut into quarters

4 fresh figs, cut into quarters

2 teaspoons sugar

2 teaspoons ground cinnamon

1–2 tablespoons runny honey

sea salt

2 teaspoons sesame seeds, toasted, to serve

Plain, Buttery Couscous (see page 77), to serve (optional)

a roasting tray with rack (trivet)

Serves 4

Using a mortar and pestle, pound the ginger with the garlic and a little salt to form a paste. Beat 2 tablespoons of the oil into the paste. Make incisions all over the duck legs using a sharp knife. Put the legs in a dish and rub the oil and ginger mixture all over them, making sure you get it into the incisions. Cover and chill in the refrigerator for at least 2 hours.

Preheat the oven to 200°C (400°F) Gas 6. Transfer the marinated duck legs to a rack in a roasting tray and roast them in the oven for about 30 minutes, until golden.

Remove the duck legs from the oven and drain off any excess fat. Tip 1 tablespoon of the duck fat into a heavy-based saucepan and stir in the pears and figs. Sprinkle the sugar and cinnamon over the fruit and cook for 2–3 minutes, until slightly caramelized.

Transfer the duck legs to the roasting dish and surround them with the pears and figs. Drizzle the honey over the duck and return it to the oven. Roast for a further 10 minutes, then serve immediately with the sesame seeds sprinkled over the top.

vegetables, side dishes and preserves

baked stuffed aubergines
aubergines farcies

When they are in season, there is often an aubergine dish on the table. Versatile and filling, aubergines are used in many ways, as side dishes, snacks, main courses and even dessert. This dish of baked stuffed aubergines can be served as a course on its own or as a side dish to roasted and grilled meats.

2 aubergines, halved lengthways

2–3 tablespoons olive oil, plus extra
for drizzling

1 onion, chopped

2 tomatoes, skinned and chopped plus 1
tomato, skinned and thinly sliced

2 garlic cloves, crushed

50 g fresh breadcrumbs, toasted

a small bunch of fresh coriander, chopped

1–2 teaspoons Harissa (see page 11)

1 teaspoon sugar

sea salt and freshly ground black pepper

Serves 4

Preheat the oven to 180ºC (350ºF) Gas 4. Using a spoon, scoop out the aubergine flesh and place it on a chopping board. Brush the insides of the empty aubergine shells with a little olive oil, place them on a baking tray and bake them into the oven for 4–5 minutes.

Meanwhile, coarsely chop the aubergine flesh. Heat the remaining oil in a pan and fry the onions to soften. Add the aubergine flesh, cook for a few minutes more then stir in the tomatoes. Add the garlic, breadcrumbs, coriander, harissa and sugar. Season to taste with salt and pepper.

Spoon the mixture into the empty aubergine shells. Arrange the slices of tomato on the top of each one, drizzle with a little olive oil and bake in the preheated oven for 20–25 minutes. Serve hot.

Casablancan stuffed tomatoes
tomates farcies

In season, there is such an abundance of sun-ripened tomatoes that they are used in salads, added to couscous, tagines, roasted, grilled or stuffed. In Casablanca, these tomatoes stuffed with couscous and herbs are popular as a starter, or they are served on their own with a salad – a common sight on the *pied-noir* table.

150 g couscous

½ teaspoon salt

150 ml warm water

3–4 tablespoons olive oil, plus extra
for drizzling

4 large tomatoes

1 onion, finely chopped

1 carrot, peeled and diced

a sprinkling of sugar

1–2 teaspoons Ras-el-hanout (see page 93)

a bunch each of fresh flat leaf parsley and
fresh coriander, finely chopped

½ preserved lemon, finely chopped (see
page 11)

sea salt and freshly ground black pepper

Serves 4

Preheat the oven to 180ºC (350ºF) Gas 4. Put the couscous in a bowl. Stir the salt into the warm water and pour it over the couscous, stirring all the time so that the water is absorbed evenly. Leave the couscous to swell for about 10 minutes before using your fingers to rub 1 tablespoon of the oil into the couscous grains to break up the lumps and aerate them.

Slice the top off each tomato and set aside. Using a spoon, scoop out the pulp and seeds and reserve in a bowl. In a heavy-based saucepan, heat the remaining olive oil and stir in the onion and carrot. Fry until they begin to caramelize, then stir in the tomato pulp and sugar. Add the ras-el-hanout and cook until the mixture forms a thick sauce. Season to taste with salt and pepper.

Tip the spicy tomato mixture onto the couscous and mix well. Add the fresh herbs and preserved lemon and toss until it is thoroughly combined. Spoon the couscous into each tomato cavity and place a top on each one like a lid. Put the filled tomatoes in a baking dish, drizzle with a little olive oil and bake in the preheated oven for about 25 minutes. Serve hot or leave to cool and eat them at room temperature.

spicy potato omelette
mhemmer

4–6 medium potatoes, unpeeled and halved

1 teaspoon sea salt

6–8 eggs

1 teaspoon ground turmeric

1 teaspoon ground cumin

1 teaspoon paprika

½ teaspoon ground coriander

a small bunch of fresh flat leaf parsley, finely chopped

1 tablespoon olive oil

sea salt and freshly ground black pepper

Serve 4–6

This Spanish-style potato omelette can be cut into thin strips and served as a starter, or divided into segments and presented as a snack or as a side dish with grilled food. The entire omelette can be cooked on the stove and browned under the grill, or it can be baked in the oven.

Put the potatoes in a saucepan with plenty of water and bring to the boil. Add the salt and boil the potatoes until soft enough to mash. Drain and refresh under cold running water. Peel off the skins, transfer the potatoes to a bowl and mash them. Beat the eggs into the potatoes and add the spices and parsley. Season to taste with salt and pepper.

Heat the oil in a heavy-based frying pan, then tip in the potato mixture making sure it spreads evenly in the pan. Cover and cook over low heat for 10–15 minutes, until the omelette has puffed up and is firm to the touch. Place the pan under a preheated medium/hot grill for 3–4 minutes to brown the top of the omelette. Cut the omelette into strips or segments to serve.

sautéed spinach with orange and almonds
sauté d'épinards

This dish is generally made with spinach or mallow, which grows wild in the countryside and is picked for vegetable dishes and soup. Quite often you will come across makeshift stalls selling bunches of mallow by the dusty roadside.

500 g fresh spinach leaves, thoroughly rinsed and drained

2–3 tablespoons olive oil and a nut of butter

1 onion, roughly chopped

2 garlic cloves, finely chopped

freshly squeezed juice and rind of 1 orange

2 tablespoons flaked almonds, toasted

sea salt and freshly ground black pepper

Serves 2–4

Put the spinach in a steamer and cook for 8–10 minutes, until soft. Tip the cooked spinach onto a wooden board and chop to a pulp. Set aside. Heat the oil and butter in a heavy-based saucepan. Stir in the onion and garlic and cook until they begin to colour. Add the spinach and mix until thoroughly combined. Add the orange juice and rind and season to taste with salt and pepper. Tip the spinach into a serving dish and garnish with the toasted almonds.

braised fennel and courgette with aniseed
fenouil et courgette braisés

Braised vegetables, such as courgettes and artichokes, are often combined with fruit or spices and served as accompaniment to tagines or roasted meats. This *pied-noir* recipe from Casablanca is light and aromatic rather than spicy and complements the varied fish tagines.

3–4 tablespoons olive oil

2 fennel bulbs, trimmed and chopped

2 medium courgettes, trimmed and cubed

1 tablespoon butter

2 teaspoons aniseeds

½ preserved lemon, very thinly sliced (see page 11)

sea salt and freshly ground black pepper

Serves 4

Heat the oil in a heavy-based pan and stir in the fennel. Cover with a lid and cook gently for 10–15 minutes. Stir in the courgettes and cook for a further 5 minutes, until they begin to soften.

Add the butter and the aniseeds and toss thoroughly. Season to taste with salt and pepper, sprinkle with the preserved lemon and serve immediately.

honey-glazed pumpkin with spices
ambassel mechoui

700 g pumpkin flesh, with skin and seeds removed

50 g butter

2–3 tablespoons runny honey

2 cinnamon sticks

3–4 cloves

1 teaspoon ground ginger

½ teaspoon cayenne

a small bunch of fresh coriander, finely chopped

sea salt and freshly ground black pepper

an ovenproof baking dish

Serves 4

Root vegetables and members of the squash family, such as sweet potatoes, turnips, butternut and pumpkins, are often cooked with honey and spices as their sweet flesh remains succulent and marries well with the flavours. Generally, these side dishes are served with grilled or roasted meats.

Preheat the oven to 180°C (350°F) Gas 4. Put the pumpkin in a steamer and cook for about 10 minutes, until the flesh is tender but still firm. Tip the steamed flesh into an ovenproof dish.

Melt the butter in a saucepan and stir in the honey. Add the cinnamon sticks, cloves, ground ginger and cayenne and season to taste with salt and pepper. Pour the mixture over the pumpkin then bake in the preheated oven for 15–20 minutes.

Tip the glazed pumpkin onto a serving plate, remove the cinnamon and cloves, then sprinkle with the coriander. Serve warm as a side dish to roasted or grilled chicken or meat.

Moroccan ratatouille with dates
sebha del hdaree

4–5 tablespoons olive oil

1 onion, halved lengthways and
sliced crossways

2 garlic cloves, chopped

1 red pepper, halved lengthways and sliced
crossways, with stalk and seeds removed

1 medium aubergine, halved lengthways and
sliced crossways

2 courgettes, sliced

225 g stoned, ready-to-eat dates,
halved lengthways

2 x 400 g tins of chopped tomatoes

1–2 teaspoons sugar

2 teaspoons Ras-el-hanout (see page 93)

a small bunch of fresh flat leaf parsley,
coarsely chopped

sea salt and freshly ground black pepper

Serves 4–6

Similar to a French ratatouille, this delicious dish is spiked with a touch of
ras-el-hanout and sweetened with succulent dates. It can be served with bread
or couscous, or as an accompaniment to a tagine, grilled meats or fish.

Heat the oil in a tagine or a heavy-based casserole. Stir in the onion and garlic and cook
for 2–3 minutes until they begin to soften. Add the pepper, aubergine and courgettes and
cook for a further 3–4 minutes. Add the dates, tomatoes, sugar and ras-el-hanout and mix
thoroughly. Cover with a lid and cook for about 40 minutes, until the vegetables are tender.

Season to taste with salt and pepper. Sprinkle the chopped parsley over the top and serve
the ratatouille hot.

green leaf and herb jam with olives
la confiture d'herbes

You can use any green leafy vegetables, such as spinach, kale, celery and broccoli leaves combined with fresh coriander and flat leaf parsley to make this tasty Moroccan dish, which is flavoured with a hint of smoked paprika. The prepared jam will keep in the refrigerator in an airtight container, with a layer of olive oil on top, for 4–5 days. Serve it as a dip with crudités or flat bread, or as a condiment with grilled meat, poultry or fish.

Put the spinach and celery leaves in a steamer and cook until soft. Refresh the leaves under cold running water, drain well and squeeze out the excess water. Transfer the steamed leaves to a wooden board and chop to a pulp.

Heat 2 tablespoons olive oil in the base of a tagine or in a heavy-based casserole. Stir in the garlic and cumin seeds until they emit a nutty aroma. Stir in the olives, parsley and coriander and add the paprika. Toss in the pulped spinach and celery leaves and cook over gentle heat for about 10 minutes, until the mixture is smooth and compact. Season to taste with salt and pepper and leave to cool.

Tip the leaf and herb jam into a bowl and bind with the remaining tablespoon of olive oil and the lemon juice.

225 g baby spinach leaves
a handful of celery leaves
3 tablespoons olive oil
2–3 garlic cloves, crushed
1 teaspoon cumin seeds
6–8 black olives, stoned and finely chopped
a large bunch each of fresh flat leaf parsley and fresh coriander, finely chopped
1 teaspoon Spanish smoked paprika
freshly squeezed juice of ½ lemon
sea salt and freshly ground black pepper

Serves 4

mixed salad pickles
torshi

One of the most colourful sights in the souks of Fes and Marrakesh are the stacked jars of pickles and preserves. In addition to the ubiquitous preserved lemons, there are a variety of vegetables and fruit such as bitter oranges, aubergines, turnips, radishes, peaches, cucumber and beetroot. Often mildly spiced, or spiked with garlic, and sometimes coloured with saffron, pickles and preserves are generally served as a starter alongside other salads, or they are enjoyed as a snack with savoury pastries, *brochettes* or *merguez* sausages. These salad pickles can be made the day before eating, or they can be stored in a jar in the refrigerator for up to 2 weeks.

2 medium carrots, peeled and cut into matchsticks

1–2 white radishes, peeled and cut into matchsticks

1 small cucumber, peeled, deseeded and cut into matchsticks

1 red pepper, deseeded and cut into matchsticks

a few generous pinches of sea salt

2 tablespoons blanched almonds

2 teaspoons pink peppercorns

1–2 teaspoons cumin seeds

a pinch of saffron fronds

1–2 cinnamon sticks

freshly squeezed juice of 2–3 lemons

1 tablespoon white vinegar

2 tablespoons sugar

1–2 tablespoons orange flower water

a small bunch of fresh coriander, finely chopped

Serves 4–6

Put all the vegetables in a bowl and sprinkle with the salt. Leave to weep for about 30 minutes, then rinse and drain thoroughly.

Tip the vegetables back into the bowl and add the almonds, peppercorns, cumin seeds, saffron and cinnamon sticks. Add the lemon juice, vinegar and sugar and mix well. Cover the bowl and chill in the refrigerator for 6 hours, or overnight.

Before serving, stir in the orange flower water and coriander. Serve the pickles at room temperature.

sweet snacks, desserts and drinks

sweet couscous with cinnamon and pistachios
kesksou seffa

175 g golden raisins or sultanas

300 ml warm tea (made with green or black tea leaves)

450 g fine couscous

600 ml boiling water

a pinch of salt

1–2 tablespoons sunflower oil

1–2 tablespoons sugar

2–3 tablespoons orange flower water

1 tablespoon ground cinnamon

25 g butter

2 tablespoons shelled, unsalted pistachios

2 tablespoons icing sugar

4 tablespoons runny honey

4–6 tablespoons single or double cream

Serves 4–6

This traditional dish of sweet couscous is one of the most popular snacks and is often served at religious festivals. It is also enjoyed as a nourishing breakfast, served warm or at room temperature. Other dried fruits and nuts, such as apricots, almonds and pine nuts, can be added to the couscous.

Put the raisins in a heatproof bowl and pour in the warm tea. Leave the raisins to soak for about 1 hour, until they are nice and plump, then drain them thoroughly. Put the couscous in a separate heatproof bowl and pour in the boiling water with a pinch of salt. Cover the bowl and leave for 10–15 minutes, until the couscous has absorbed all the water. Drizzle the oil over the couscous and, using your fingertips, rub it in to separate and aerate the grains. Add the sugar, orange flower water and half the cinnamon to the couscous. Stir in the soaked raisins and then pack the mixture into a smaller bowl, so that it all fits in snuggly. Invert the bowl onto a serving plate, so that you have a couscous dome.

Melt the butter in a frying pan, add the pistachios and stir for 1–2 minutes, until they emit a nutty aroma. Scatter the pistachios over and around the couscous dome. Decorate the couscous by rubbing the remaining cinnamon between your thumb and index finger to create lines. Sift the icing sugar over the top and around the base. Heat the honey and drizzle it over the couscous. Serve with a jug of cream for pouring.

Said to resemble the horns of the antelope that roam the Atlas mountains, these sickle-moon shaped pastries are a delightful treat. Traditionally, they are served as a gift to guests with a glass of mint tea or a cold drink, such as almond milk, but they are also available in the street pastry shops to munch on at any time of day.

gazelle's horns
kaab el ghzal

250 g plain flour, plus extra for dusting

a pinch of salt

2 tablespoons sunflower oil, plus extra for brushing

100 ml orange flower water, plus extra for sprinkling

100 ml water

icing sugar, for dusting

For the almond filling:

300 g ground almonds

300 g caster sugar

2 eggs, lightly beaten

3–4 tablespoons orange flower water

1 teaspoon ground cinnamon

a fluted pastry wheel

a baking tray, lightly oiled

Makes 25–30 pastries

Preheat the oven to 180°C (350°F) Gas 4. First, prepare the filling. Put all the filling ingredients in a wide-rimmed bowl and, using your hand, work them into a stiff paste. Take a small portion of the mixture into your hands and roll it into a log, approximately 8 cm long. Continue with the rest of the mixture until you have 25–30 logs. Brush them lightly with the oil as you make them so that they remain moist. Set aside.

To prepare the pastry dough, sift the flour and salt into a bowl. Make a well in the centre and pour in the sunflower oil, orange flower water and water. Using your fingers, draw in the flour from the outside of the bowl to form a dough. Knead the dough with your hand for about 10 minutes, until it is soft and springy.

Transfer the dough to a lightly floured surface and roll it out to form a large rectangle, about 2 mm thick. Place 3 almond logs along the long side, 5 cm from the edge and leaving a 5 cm gap between them. Brush the edges of the pastry and around the almond logs with a little water. Fold the edge over the almond logs and press the dough around the filling to keep it in place. Using a fluted pastry wheel, carefully cut a half moon, starting from the folded edge, around the filling, and back down to the folded edge again, so that you end up with three half circles. Repeat with the rest of the pastry, until you have roughly 25 half–circle shaped pastries. Place a finger in the middle of the bottom edge of each pastry and, carefully, press the filling upwards to shape the pastry into a crescent moon, or a gazelle's horn.

Place the gazelle's horns onto a lightly oiled baking tray and prick each one with a fork. Bake them in the preheated oven for 15–20 minutes until lightly browned. Transfer them to a wire rack, brush with a little orange flower water and dust with icing sugar while still hot. Serve warm or at room temperature.

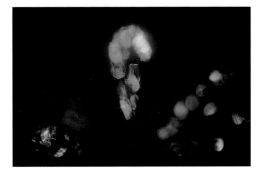

Coiled like a snake, this is the most stunning of Morocco's sweet pastries and one that you should not leave the country without tasting. Literally translated from Arabic as 'snake', *m'hanncha* is crisp and buttery and filled with an exquisite scented almond paste. The layers of pastry are made using the thin sheets of *ouarka*, which can be substituted with filo. Traditionally *m'hanncha* is prepared in large quantities to be served on festive occasions, accompanied by a glass of mint tea or almond milk.

classic 'snake' pastry with almond filling
m'hanncha

125 g filo (about 5–6 sheets)
60 g butter, melted
1 egg yolk, mixed with 1 tablespoon water

For the almond filling:
350 g ground almonds
225 g caster sugar
50 g icing sugar
1 tablespoon ground cinnamon, plus extra for decorating
2–3 tablespoons orange flower water
2–3 tablespoons icing sugar, plus extra for sprinkling
2 teaspoons ground cinnamon

a round baking tin or wide baking tray

Serves 8–10

Preheat the oven to 180°C (350°F) Gas 4. To make the filling, put all the ingredients for the filling in a large bowl and work them with your hands to form a stiff paste. Take a lump of the paste out of the bowl and roll it on a flat surface to form a finger that is roughly 1.5 cm thick and about 8 cm long. Repeat with the remaining filling. Cover and chill in the refrigerator for 30 minutes.

Line a round baking tin or a wide baking tray, with a piece of foil then place it and the filo sheets beside your work surface. Make sure you keep the filo in a stack covered with a damp cloth, while working with them. Take the first sheet of filo and place it on the surface in front of you, with the longer side nearest to you. Lightly brush the top of it with a little butter and place several of the almond fingers, end to end, along the edge nearest to you. Roll the nearest edge up over the filling, tuck in the ends, and roll it into a long, thin tube. Gently push both ends of the tube towards the centre so that it creases like an accordion then place it on the foil in the middle of the baking tin. Carefully, curve it around into a tight coil.

Repeat the process with the other sheets of filo, until all the almond mixture fingers are used up and the pastry resembles a coiled snake. Brush the top of the pastry with the egg yolk mixture and bake it in the oven for 30–35 minutes, until crisp and lightly browned.

Take the pastry out of the oven and sprinkle it liberally with icing sugar. Decorate the top by rubbing the ground cinnamon between your thumb and index finger to create thin lines from the centre to the outer rim of the pastry snake, like the spokes of a wheel. Serve while still warm, or at room temperature.

semolina pancakes with honey
beghrir

These light, airy pancakes are a great favourite for breakfast or a sweet snack. Bubbly on one side, smooth on the other, they melt deliciously in the mouth with a drizzle of honey, lashings of butter or a sprinkling of sugar and cinnamon.

15 g fresh yeast
125 ml lukewarm water
225 g fine semolina
250 g plain flour
½ teaspoon sea salt
2 eggs
125 ml lukewarm milk
sunflower oil, for shallow frying
50 g unsalted butter
200 ml scented runny honey

Makes 12–16 pancakes

Put the yeast in a bowl with the lukewarm water and leave it in a warm place until it dissolves and becomes frothy.

Sift the semolina, flour and salt into a large bowl. Make a well in the centre. Beat the eggs into the milk and pour the mixture into the well. Tip in the yeast mixture and, using a wooden spoon, draw in the flour from the sides of the bowl. Beat the mixture for about 5 minutes, until light and smooth. Cover the bowl with a clean tea towel and leave to prove in a warm place for at least 2 hours.

To make the pancakes, heat a non-stick frying pan and wipe it with a little oil. Pour a small ladleful of batter into the middle of the pan and spread it a little to form a thick round about 12–14 cm in diameter. Cook the pancake until the surface looks dry and is perforated with bubbles. Lift it out of the pan and transfer to a heated plate and cover to keep warm while you cook the remaining pancakes in the same way.

Melt the butter and heat the honey in separate pans. Drizzle the butter over the pancakes and serve immediately with the warm honey for drizzling.

dried fruit compote with orange flower water
slada fawakih bi ma z'har

250 g dried, ready-to-eat apricots
250 g stoned, ready-to-eat prunes
125 g sultanas
125 g blanched almonds
175 g cane sugar
2–3 tablespoons orange flower water
1–2 cinnamon sticks
Sweet Couscous (see page 133), Pancakes (see above) or vanilla ice cream, to serve

Serves 4–6

A wide range of delectable, juicy fruits are served fresh when ripe but, out of season, the preserved fruits are employed in infinite ways in both sweet and savoury dishes. Fruit compotes are popular at any time of day, starting with breakfast or a mid-morning snack, as a dessert or even as a palate cleanser between courses.

Put the dried fruit and almonds in a bowl and pour in just enough water to cover. Gently stir in the sugar and orange flower water and add the cinnamon stick. Cover the bowl and chill it in the refrigerator for 48 hours, during which time the water and sugar will form a golden syrup. Serve the chilled compote on its own, or as an accompaniment to Sweet Couscous, Pancakes or vanilla ice cream.

rose-flavoured milk pudding
muhallabia

Silky and light, this traditional pudding is a classic throughout North Africa and the Middle East, as the recipe travelled with the invading Arabs across the region. Often served at religious feasts, it can be flavoured with rosewater or orange flower water and a generous dusting of icing sugar.

60 g rice flour
1 litre whole or semi-skimmed milk
125 g caster sugar
2–3 tablespoons rosewater
1–2 tablespoons icing sugar

Serves 4–6

In a small bowl, mix the rice flour with a little of the milk to form a loose paste. Pour the rest of the milk into a heavy-based saucepan and stir in the sugar. Bring the milk to boiling point, stirring all the time, until the sugar has dissolved. Reduce the heat and stir a spoonful or two of the hot milk into the rice flour paste, then tip the mixture into the pan, stirring all the time to prevent the flour from forming lumps. Bring the milk back to boiling point and stir in the rosewater. Reduce the heat to low and simmer gently for 20–25 minutes, stirring from time to time, until the mixture becomes quite thick and coats the back of the spoon.

Pour the mixture into a large serving bowl, or individual ones, and leave to cool, allowing a skin to form on top. Chill in the refrigerator and, just before serving, dust with icing sugar.

watermelon salad with rosewater and lemon balm
slada bil dellah

1 ripe watermelon, or a large wedge, weighing about 1.5 kg

2 teaspoons sugar

3–4 tablespoons rosewater

a small bunch of fresh lemon balm

Serves 4–6

In many Moroccan households when fresh fruit is served at the end of a meal it is usually presented as a salad, or displayed decoratively on a traditional platter. Chopped nuts or fresh herbs, such as lemon balm or mint, are often scattered over the fruit, honey is occasionally drizzled over tart fruit, and the classic rose- and orange flower waters are added for a splash of extra flavour.

Remove the skin and seeds from the watermelon. Put the flesh on a plate to catch the juice and cut it into bite-sized cubes. Tip the cubes into a serving bowl or shallow dish and pour over the juice.

Stir the sugar into the rosewater, until it has dissolved, and pour the scented mixture over the watermelon. Toss the watermelon lightly, cover the bowl with clingfilm and chill it in the refrigerator for at least 1 hour.

Toss the watermelon once more before serving, scatter the lemon balm leaves over the top and serve chilled or at room temperature.

candied baby aubergines
aubergines glacées

The tradition of candied fruit and vegetables is popular throughout North Africa and the Middle East, where the variety ranges from watermelon, plum tomatoes, carrots, quinces, grapefruit peel, clementines, lemons, sweet potatoes, courgettes and baby aubergines. The baby aubergines are my favourite and are delicious served as a treat at the end of a special meal with a glass of mint tea.

8–12 firm baby aubergines, stalk intact
225 ml water
450 g caster sugar
freshly squeezed juice of 1 lemon
25 g fresh ginger, peeled and thinly sliced
2 cinnamon sticks
6 cloves
2 pieces mace
1 piece mastic* the size of a small coin

Serves 4

Prick the aubergines all over with a fork and put them in a steamer. Steam for 15 minutes, drain off any water and leave them to cool.

Meanwhile, make the syrup. Pour the water into a heavy-based saucepan. Reserve 1 teaspoon of the sugar, then add the remainder to the pan with the lemon juice. Bring the water to the boil, stirring all the time, until the sugar has dissolved. Add the spices, reduce the heat and simmer gently for 10 minutes, until the syrup is thick and coats the back of the spoon. Crush the mastic with the reserved teaspoon of sugar and stir it into the syrup.

Gently squeeze the aubergines to remove any excess water and place them in the syrup. Cook the aubergines in the syrup, partially covered, over very low heat for about 1 hour, making sure they are submerged in the syrup and that the sugar doesn't burn and catch on the bottom of the pan.

Remove the pan from the heat and leave the aubergines to cool in the syrup. Arrange the aubergines on a serving dish with the stalks pointing upwards. Strain the syrup and drizzle it over them. Alternatively, you can store the aubergines in the strained syrup in a sealed, sterilized jar for several months.

*Mastic is a resin obtained from the mastic tree, an evergreen that grows throughout the Mediterranean region. It's mainly used as a flavouring and for its 'gum' properties and is a key ingredient in Greek spoon sweets and Turkish ice cream. It can be most easily bought from specialist Greek stores as it is produced commercially for export on the Greek island of Chios.

fresh figs with walnuts and honey
yermous bil assel

Moroccans believe that figs aid digestion so, when in season, they are often served fresh at the end of a meal. There are many delicious varieties of scented honey, *assel*, in Morocco, such as thyme and lavender and the honey of 1,000 flowers (*mille-fleurs*). There is also a special honey called *jbal* that is particularly sweet and delicate as it is made by bees that only feast on figs.

4–5 tablespoons walnuts
8 fresh, ripe figs
4–5 tablespoons scented, runny honey

Serves 4

Toast the walnuts in a frying pan, or roast them on a baking tray in a medium oven, until they emit a nutty aroma and deepen in colour. Using a mortar and pestle, or an electric blender, grind the walnuts coarsely.

Using a sharp knife, slit open each fig by cutting it from the top into quarters, but make sure you don't cut through the base, so that the fruit opens like a flower. Arrange the figs on a serving dish. Drizzle the honey over each one and scatter the toasted walnuts over the fruit and around the dish. Serve immediately.

date, pistachio and coconut truffles
tmar kweerat

The nomadic Berbers rely heavily on dates as a main source of food and many traditional dishes include them – lamb tagines, couscous and a variety of sweetmeats, such as these truffles. Some modern cooks tuck these succulent truffles into oven-baked lamb tagines but, generally, in the home, they are one of the sweetmeats traditionally offered to guests with a glass of mint tea as a mark of hospitality.

250 g shelled pistachios
250 g stoned dates, roughly chopped
1–2 tablespoons orange flower water
1–2 teaspoons ground cinnamon
1 tablespoon honey
200 g desiccated coconut

15–20 miniature fluted paper cases (optional)

Makes 15–20 small truffles

Toast the pistachios in a heavy-based frying pan, or roast them in a medium oven on a baking tray, until they emit a lovely nutty aroma. Using a mortar and pestle, or an electric blender, grind the pistachios. Add the dates and pound them with the ground pistachios to form a thick paste.

Spoon the date and pistachio paste into a bowl and, using your hands, mix in the orange flower water, cinnamon and honey. Shape the mixture into 15–20 small, bite-sized balls. Sprinkle the coconut onto a plate or flat surface and then roll the sticky balls in it, until they are evenly coated.

Arrange the truffles in a serving dish or place them in miniature fluted paper cases. They can be stored in an airtight container in the refrigerator for 1 week. Serve them at room temperature.

fluffy pistachio nougat
jabane

A variety of soft and hard nougats, made with sesame seeds, sunflower seeds, peanuts, almonds, pistachios and pumpkin seeds, are sold in the streets and souks. This soft nougat, which employs mastic for its chewy twang and mild, resinous flavour, is traditionally served in Jewish households to celebrate the end of Passover but, throughout Morocco it is hugely popular with children.

300 g shelled, unsalted pistachios

300 ml water

900 g caster sugar

1 piece mastic the size of a small coin (see page 145)

freshly squeezed juice of 2 lemons

4 egg whites

2 tablespoons shelled, unsalted pistachios, finely ground, to decorate (optional)

Serves 8–10

Toast the pistachios in a heavy-based frying pan, or roast them in a medium oven on a baking tray, until they emit a lovely nutty aroma. Using a mortar and pestle, or an electric blender, crush the roasted pistachios coarsely.

Pour the water into a heavy-based saucepan. Reserve 1 teaspoon of the sugar and add the remainder to the pan. Bring the mixture to the boil, stirring all the time, until the sugar has dissolved. Reduce the heat and simmer gently for about 10 minutes, until the syrup coats the back of the wooden spoon – the syrup should be thick and transparent.

Using a small mortar and pestle, grind the mastic with the reserved teaspoon of sugar and add it with the lemon juice to the syrup. Take the pan off the heat and cool the syrup down by beating it continuously, until warm to the touch.

Whisk the egg whites in a bowl, until thick and frothy and then fold them, one spoonful at a time, into the warm syrup. Place the pan over low heat and stir for 5 minutes. Gradually add the crushed pistachios, making sure they are well dispersed throughout the mixture. Tip the mixture into a large serving bowl, or individual serving bowls, and leave to cool. Decorate with a sprinkling of finely ground pistachios and serve the jabane while it is still just warm, or at room temperature.

quince jam
confiture de coings

As quince jam is enjoyed throughout the Middle East and North Africa, it probably arrived in Morocco with the invading Arabs. Sweet fruit preserves, such as green fig, bitter orange and quince are also a feature of *pied-noir* and Jewish cooking. The kitchen fills with a lovely floral aroma as the fruit is poached in an aromatic syrup, which results in a conserve, rather than a spreadable jam, that is enjoyed with bread, semolina buns and pancakes, milk pudding and yoghurt.

500 g fresh quinces
450 g caster sugar
250 ml water
2 cinnamon sticks
1 vanilla pod
2–3 star anise
6 cloves
2 strips of lemon peel

Makes 2–3 jam jars

Peel and core the quince and pop them into a bowl of water as you do each one to prevent them from discolouring.

Put the sugar and water in a heavy-based saucepan and bring to the boil, stirring all the time, until the sugar has dissolved. Add the spices and lemon peel, reduce the heat and simmer gently while you grate the quince, or dice it. Add the quince to the syrup and simmer gently for about 25 minutes.

Leave the quince jam to cool in the pan. Remove the lemon peel and spices and spoon the jam into sterilized jars. Seal the lids tightly and store for several months.

almond milk
hlib b'louz

Almond milk is a classic North African and Middle Eastern drink. Served chilled on a hot day, it is both nourishing and refreshing. Traditionally, the 'milk' is extracted from the almonds but modern recipes often add cow's milk. In Morocco, orange flower water or fresh orange rind are added to the drink to give it a floral or zesty lift and, on special occasions, rose petals are floated on the surface of each glass.

250 g blanched almonds
125 g caster sugar
600 ml water
1–2 tablespoons orange flower water
rose petals, orange zest or ground cinnamon, to serve

Serves 4

Using a mortar and pestle, or an electric blender, pound the almonds with half the sugar to a smooth paste – add a splash of water if the paste gets too stiff.

Put the water and the remaining sugar in a heavy-based saucepan and bring it to the boil, stirring until the sugar has dissolved. Stir in the almond paste and simmer for 5 minutes.

Turn off the heat and stir in the orange flower water. Leave the mixture to cool in the pan to enable the flavours to mingle. Once cool, strain the mixture through a muslin cloth, or a fine, plastic sieve (don't use a metal one as it will taint the flavour and colour of the almonds). Use your hand to squeeze all the milk out of the almonds.

Pour the cloudy liquid into a jug and chill in the refrigerator. When ready to serve, give it a stir and pour the milk into glasses over ice cubes, or place the glasses in the freezer so they are frosty when served. Decorate with rose petals, a fine curl of orange peel, or a pinch of ground cinnamon.

hospitality and mint tea

When I took my children up to the Kasbah Toubkal, a magnificent mountain retreat in the Atlas Mountains, the climb was not difficult, but it was hot, making it seem more tiring than it really was. Fortunately my children were transported by mule and blissfully unaware of the draining heat, but I was thankful when we arrived at the walls of the ancient refuge. In the shelter and shade of the pretty courtyard and gardens, the welcome was delightful – a cool sprinkling of refreshing scented water splashed on the hands and face and the most succulent dates I have ever tasted dipped in a bowl of milk – a traditional Berber offering to welcome guests.

Hospitality is of utmost importance in Morocco. Offering, sharing and receiving are intertwined and, even in the humblest of homes, a visitor will be offered milk and dates, or a simple glass of milk flavoured with rosewater, sometimes with the additional decorative touch of floating rose petals, or a steaming glass of refreshing mint tea. Bread and olives, or sweetmeats and fruit, may also be offered to welcome guests into a home. When cooking for guests, it is customary to make vast quantities of food so that the guests will be completely satisfied and unable to finish. A meal can take several hours to prepare and the women of the house may be absent from the social gathering for the duration of the cooking as several soups, steaming tagines, roasted meat, vegetables or salads, couscous and fruit all need to be prepared.

As eating is regarded as an art and a pleasure, there is no hurry. In most homes, it is customary to eat using your hands so, at the start of a meal and during it, a jug of perfumed water is passed around to refresh the face and fingers of the right hand. If you have never tried eating with your hands, it is in fact very pleasurable as it enables you to appreciate the texture of the food as well as the flavour. However, you must remember to use the right hand, and you don't just shove your hand into the food and stuff it into your mouth. There is a skill, which can take some time to perfect, in rolling couscous into a little ball and placing it into the mouth without even touching the lips. As dish follows dish, it is vital to pace yourself and eat slowly so that you can enjoy each mouthful. Burping at the end of a meal is regarded as a sign of appreciation for all the good food and hospitality – it is customary to follow it with the words 'nhemdou Allah', 'we praise God' – and it is a cue for the food to be cleared and for the diners to recline on cushions while the mint tea is served.

A glass of mint tea is the essence of Moroccan hospitality and it is bad manners to refuse one. Although the making and offering of tea is regarded as an institution in Morocco, it only arrived in North Africa in 1854 during the Crimean War, when British merchants were hindered by the blockade in the Baltic and had to seek new markets, such as Tangier, for their goods, which included tea from China. Prior to this period, Moroccans had drunk simple infusions of wormwood, saffron and herbs, including mint. When the leaders of different Berber tribes met to discuss a dispute, an elaborate tea ceremony would be held using decorative samovars and glasses.

Nowadays, the ubiquitous sweet mint tea of Morocco is the national drink. It is drunk at any time of day and is offered wherever you go throughout the country. The only variation is in the south of Morocco, particularly in the saffron-growing region around Taliouine, where saffron tea is offered. In imperial circles and on refined occasions a special infusion may be prepared with balls of amber, but this is very rare. Otherwise, it is mint tea, *atay bi na'na'*, in the morning, during the day and at night. It is served as a welcome drink, it is offered while conducting business or bargaining in the souks, it is drunk to quench the thirst on a hot day and it is always served as a digestive at the end of a meal.

The art of tea making is steeped in ritual, but it is not complicated. In fact it is a charming process with a great deal of ceremony in the brewing and pouring. Traditionally, ornate samovars were used but nowadays they are generally reserved for elaborate tea ceremonies and feasts. Instead, a fine steel-plated, bulbous-shaped teapot is used and sugar is added to the pot rather than the glasses, so that the tea is served sweet. Sugar is generally chipped off a cone-shaped cane loaf and added liberally to the pot. The sweet-toothed Moroccans do not skimp on the sugar which enhances the flavour of the mint, masking the bitterness of the green tea leaves. Generally, fresh scented mint, and lots of it, is used – perfectionists use the variety *Mentha viridis* as it is strongly scented – but an aromatic garden mint imparts a good flavour. When in season, orange blossom is added to give the tea a refreshing floral lift and, occasionally, dried mint is infused in the winter versions, which may include other herbs such as sage and thyme, and dried rose and geranium petals.

The making of mint tea is regarded as a 'gift of God'. There aren't really any rules or precise proportions, just the inherent know-how, as each pot of tea should be personal and taste different. To make the tea, the teapot is first warmed with boiling water by swirling it around and then tipping it out. The green tea is added to the pot, followed by a large handful of fresh mint leaves on their stalks and the sugar. The boiling water is poured in and stirred once to help dissolve the sugar and, once the mint leaves rise to the surface, the tea is left to infuse for five minutes. The tea is generally drunk from small, ornate glasses, often in little holders. As the tea is poured, the teapot is held close to the glass and gradually raised higher and higher to create a sense of ceremony as well as a little froth on top of each glass. On festive occasions two teapots, one in each hand, will be held above the glass to be raised with a skilful flourish that creates a thick froth on top.

websites
and mail order

Note: this book uses the Anglicized spellings of Marrakesh and Fes. Where Marrakech is spelt with a 'c' in a website address this is an alternative spelling and still correct.

COOKING SCHOOLS

www.holidayonthemenu.com
'Holidays for people who love food.' Learn to cook Moroccan food within the walls of the old medina in Marrakesh with a 'dada' as your teacher. See website for full details.

www.rhodeschoolofcuisine.com
Tel: + 44 (0) 207 193 1221
'International cooking schools for the gourmet traveller.' This UK-based company offers Moroccan cookery courses at a luxury villa just outside the ancient city of Marrakesh. See website for full details.

Centre de Qualification Hotelière et Touristique de Touarga-Rabat
Set up nearly 20 years ago by King Hassan, this is a cookery academy run by women for women. The school is dedicated to teaching the traditions of Morocco's cooking and turning out graduates who will travel across the world to show off their nation's food. To arrange a group visit, contact The Moroccan National Tourist office in London on 020 7437 0073 or via their website (see Useful Information, right).

SHOPPING

www.seasonedpioneers.co.uk
Seasoned Pioneers
Tel: 0800 068 2348 (Freephone)
This innovative company sources and sells authentic, specialist seasonings. Highly commended by many leading food writers and chefs they source and sell authentic seasonings from each corner of the globe. They make truly excellent ras-el-hanout and zahtar, both available to order on-line.

www.thespiceshop.co.uk
The Spice Shop
1 Blenheim Crescent
London W11 2EE
Tel: + 44 (0) 207 221 4448
info@thespiceshop.co.uk
This delightful shop in the bustling heart of Notting Hill and near the world famous Portobello Road Market, sells a wide range of herbs, spice blends, nuts and dried fruit. They stock argan oil, rose petals and homemade preserved lemons, available to order on-line.

www.maroque.co.uk
An on-line shopping site selling all things Moroccan, such as traditional tableware (including both cooking and serving tagines) plus authentic ingredients such as preserved lemons, ras-el-hanout, mint tea, orange flower water, rosewater and couscous. They also stock a range of argan oil bath and body products from Les Sens de Marrakesh.

www.kazzbar.co.uk
An on-line shopping site selling a good selection of attractive, contemporary Moroccan pottery, ceramics and glassware, including unusual stemmed tea glasses, as well as the more traditional ones in a range of colours.

www.lecreuset.com
Le Creuset make a tagine that is perfect for use on a gas or electric hob as it consists of an enamelled cast iron base with a glazed earthenware lid (see page 57). Visit their website for details of the range of colours available and stockists worldwide.

www.moroccanbazaar.co.uk
Tel: 020 8575 1818
A wholesale supplier and importer of furniture and home accessories from Morocco. They also offer a full rental service of Moroccan seating, furniture, rugs and lamps etc. all available to hire for private parties, weddings and other special occasions. See website for details of their London showroom.

Twizra
Rue Bab Agnaou
South Medina
Marrakesh
Morocco
twizra@hotmail.com
If you love to shop, but hate haggling over prices, then visit this wonderful shop in Marrakesh – three floors of jewellery, ceramics, furniture and babouches with no pressure-selling and as much mint tea as you can drink. A great place to buy collectable kitchen utensils.

La Kasbah de Teifirt
Km 39, 7 Imin Oumassin
Ourika
Marrakesh
Morocco
Tel: + 212 66 01 24 69
Traditional carpets and decorative art from the Atlas Mountains.

Caverne d'Ali Baba
Fhal Chidmi 17(A)
El Mouassine
Marrakesh
Morocco
Tel: + 212 44 44 21 48
A huge selection of decorative ceramics.

Touareg Chez Sidammed
Fhal Chidmi Rue Lamoissine
Kissariat Lamoisni
Marrakesh 6/7 40000
Morocco
Tel: + 212 62 01 34 11
Antiques and decorative art.

Cooperative Tiguemine Argan
15 km d'Essaouira
(route Marrakesh)
Morocco
Tel: + 212 24 78 49 70
Cooperative selling artisanal argan oil suitable for cooking plus a range of other products.

USEFUL INFORMATION

www.visitmorocco.org
The Moroccan National Tourist Office
The Moroccan National Tourist Office provide information on all aspects of Moroccan culture and tourism. Visit their website for general advice or contact their offices with specific enquiries.

In the UK:
205 Regent Street
London
W1B 4HB
Tel: 020 7437 0073

In Morocco:
Angle Rue Qued El Makhazine
et rue Zalaga,
BP 19 Agdal
Rabat
Morocco
Tel: + 212 537 67 40 13

www.moroccolondon.co.uk
A guide to everything Moroccan in London. Search the on-line directory for restaurants, organizations, art galleries, businesses and services, or just read articles of interest on Moroccan travel, culture and arts.

PLANNING A TRIP

www.travellink.ma
Travel Link (Morocco)
Marrakech Plaza, Nº 401
Immeuble D1
Marrakesh-Guéliz
Morocco
Tel: + 212 (0) 524 44 87 97
Based in Marrakesh, with offices in Fes and Tangier, Travel Link's English-speaking guides provide specialist tours, excursions and local sightseeing trips. See their website for full details.

www.riadmescellil.com
e-mail: riadmescellil@gmail.com
Tel: + 212 24 44 06 20
This beautiful riad in the heart of Marrakesh's medina was the location for much of the photography in this book, as well as a comfortable home to the creative team throughout the photographic shoot.

www.hipmarrakech.com
A website offering a wide selection of stylish, contemporary riad accommodation in Marrakesh.

index

acknowledgements

When researching and writing a book like this, I inevitably encounter many generous and helpful people along the way but I would particularly like to thank the team at Travel Link in Marrakesh; Ahmed Nait Taadouit, known simply as Nait, who went out of his way to accommodate my wishes and make things happen; Aziz Zrioui for patiently attending to all the details of the day-to-day arrangements; Bouazza Amri who was an excellent guide and companion to myself and my children on several excursions; and Lahcen, also known as Jelah, for guiding us in the foothills of the Atlas and leading us to the wonderful Kasbah Toubkal. I would also like to thank Taoufik Ghaffouli of La Maison Arabe and the queen of his kitchen, Laaziza Grizmi, for granting me an interview; Abderrahim Moustajidi for navigating the souks with me; and the friendly staff at Twizra, a fascinating artisan and carpet souk, where I was encouraged to part with rather a lot of money!

In London, my thanks go to Jamal el Jaidi at the Moroccan National Tourist Office and to the team at Ryland, Peters & Small: Alison Starling for commissioning me; Julia Charles, my editor, for steering the text with a keen eye; Steve Painter for the design; Peter Cassidy for the fabulous photography and Ross Dobson for the food styling.

Back home, I have my two little travelling companions, Yasmin and Zeki, to thank for their company and for their enthusiastic 'joie de vivre'. Without them travelling would be half the fun!

The publishers would like to thank Patricia Lebaud, Halima and Latifa at Riad Mesc el Lil in Marrakech, the location for much of the photography in this book and a temporary home for the creative team. For more information see page 157.